D1610136

THE IMMORTAL ISLES

THE AUTHOR AT 90

THE IMMORTAL ISLES

BY

SETON PAUL GORDON, C.B.E.

with 24 headpieces by
Finlay Mackinnon

and

37 photographs by the author

Introduction by
Dr. Adam Watson, B.Sc., Ph.D., D.Sc., F.R.S.E.

MELVEN PRESS

PERTH 1979

ISBN 0 9505884 5 8

Acknowledgments are due to W. Sinclair of Inverness for his helpful advice, Roy and Marina Dennis of Kessock for their invaluable assistance in locating the author's photographs and Dr. Adam Watson for providing the frontispiece and introduction.

First published 1926 by
Williams and Norgate, London

The Melven Press
176 High Street, Perth, Scotland
1979

Printed in Great Britain by
Billing & Sons Limited
Guildford, London and Worcester

TO THOSE WHO KNOW THE GREY WIND

CONTENTS

ERRATUM
Due to printer's error, illustrations follow page 58
and page 138.

LIST OF ILLUSTRATIONS

FOREWORD

I REGARD it as a special honour and delight to be asked to write a foreword to this, the first* of Seton Gordon's books to be republished after his death in 1977. I think it will not be the last. Seton Gordon's many books carry an ageless wonder that will continue to delight future generations of those who like the Scottish Highlands or who enjoy nature.

Books are one of the pinnacles of human culture and achievement. Few things can have a more revolutionary effect on the attitudes and beliefs of young minds in a receptive mood. That was so for me, with Seton Gordon's books. Only perhaps once or twice in a lifetime may a brief event, such as a casual glance at a book, or a sudden union of two like minds, become a clear turning point which transforms the rest of one's life. Suddenly, exciting new horizons and a whole new universe are uncovered, and one's previous existence seems dull and almost point-

* Shortly available: *Highways and Byways of the Western Highlands* (Macmillan).

less by comparison. I was eight years old, reading one of Seton Gordon's books in a library at Ballater, when such a turning point came to me. My parents had taken me to different parts of Scotland, but suddenly Deeside and the Highlands that I thought I knew were immediately relegated into distant memories of no importance. The fact was I had known them only in a superficial and trivial sense. The Highlands that Seton Gordon wrote about were utterly different, a place of endless beauty and variety with a wonderful wildlife and fine people, a place that could give infinite exploration, enjoyment and peace to human mind, soul and body. From then on I saw Scotland, its wild life, weather, skies, people and culture, with this different eye. Others whom I know had a spark lit in them by Seton Gordon's writings, and went on to become naturalists and writers themselves. And others unborn will have this magic in future.

I wrote to Seton Gordon after seeing his book, not expecting a reply from such a busy man. He replied at once, writing "It is a fine thing for you to have a love of the hills because on the hills you find yourself near grand and beautiful

things, and as you grow older you will love them
more and more." We began a regular correspon-
dence. His letters were as if written to an adult,
with not a trace of talking down to a schoolboy.

After my first exploratory letter, all my subsequent letters gave him observations of birds I
had seen, or notes on the weather, or descriptions and drawings of snow patches in summer.
I did this years before I began keeping my own
systematic records at the age of thirteen. He
appreciated this information from Aberdeenshire and the Cairngorms, as he lived in Skye
and yet still kept up a great interest in the
Deeside of his youth.

Later, I remember the intense excitement
that I had when cycling to Crathie to meet him
for the first time, at the age of 13. Next day we
went for a long walk on the hill on a fine April
day, and he showed me the first golden eagles'
eyries I had ever seen, and told me of others.
Knowing how garrulous and boastful school-
boys can be, he was right to warn me of the
dangers that the eagles would face if I told all
my friends about the exciting things I had been
doing. I kept his trust. Only a few days later, I
saw my first occupied eyrie, whose location he

had told me. This started me on the eagle observations I have continued ever since.

A romantic, Seton also had a puckish sense of humour. When I got married I saw no reason for spreading the news. Shortly before the wedding day I received a postcard, saying "Dear Adam, Is it true you are marrying a Golden Eagle—or is it only a lying rumour, and you are really engaged to the Snowy Owl of Ben MacDhui? Anyway, warm congratulations to you both. S.G.". On another occasion in the 1970s, when my father and I met him at Ballochbuie Forest, he looked at my long beard and said to me "I'm pleased to meet you for the first time. Your son here", pointing at my clean-shaven, short back-and-sides father "has been corresponding with me since he was a school-boy". A stranger might have thought Seton was just a confused old man, but the twinkle in his eye and the grin on his face told us this was another classic example of the mischievous Seton Gordon humour.

Seton Gordon maintained his great enthusi-asm into his nineties. When 90, he gave a lecture at Braemar to aid the funds of the Scottish Wildlife Trust. In an obituary for "Scottish

Birds", the journal of the Scottish Ornitholo-
gists' Club, I wrote "The slides were ancient
and blurred, but his word pictures were as good
as anything he ever wrote. Describing the dawn
sun rays catching the gold hackles on a brooding
eagle's neck, he had us there with him, over 50
years ago. Last August (1976) I spent a day with
him on the Cairngorms. Though slower, he still
had a steady step on the plateau. Remarkably,
his blue eyes sparkled as keenly as ever, and his
conversation was full of excited comments on
snow patches, birds, place names and the
Cairngorm range itself. . . ."

In the obituary I also wrote "The grand old
man has gone, on 19th March 1977 at Brackley,
Northamptonshire, only a fortnight short of 91.
With his passing ends the period of wholly exploratory naturalists in Scotland and their extraordinary breadth of interests. He was long
the last practitioner, overlapping for decades
with the modern period when scientific method
dominated ornithology. Astride two centuries,
Seton had a timeless attitude, exemplified by
the patched, decades-old kilt he wore on every
occasion, sun or snow, mansion or bothy. (My
photograph of him) might have been in Harvie-

Brown's time (late 19th century), showing nothing to indicate the real date—August 1976."

Seton's boyhood was spent at Aboyne on Deeside. He was educated privately, which doubtless accounts for the fact that his voice had no trace of the Aberdeenshire dialect and accent that one would have expected in one who was brought up in Deeside and who loved the place. After his schooling days, he went to Oxford University where he graduated in biology with honours, making a special study of the snow-patch plants of the Cairngorms. He visited the Hebrides in the first world war, when he served there as a naval patrol officer. Later, he was to make his home there for half a century. In these early years he also went to Spitsbergen on one of the early, pioneering Oxford University expeditions to the arctic.

In the "Scottish Birds" obituary I wrote "Gordon began writing articles to newspapers and magazines in his late teens, and published his first book *Birds of the Loch and Mountain* in 1907. Others soon followed. A pioneer in bird photography, he took photographs of golden eagle and greenshank that are still classics. He was also a pioneer in camping on the high tops.

These early books brimmed with enthusiasm and already showed his wide interest in birds, rare plants, snow beds, regeneration of the old Caledonian forest, piping, weather, folk lore, history, place names, the survival of Gaelic, and a deep appreciation and knowledge of the Highlands. He also described vividly some winter climbs and storms. A natural hillman, he never over-wrote the difficulties or dangers and was at home in the Cairngorms winter or summer, alone or in company."

Seton Gordon's first books were mainly on natural history and wildlife photography, but even his most specialist books on these subjects showed his sensitivity and perception of the beauty of nature, his extraordinary variety of interests, and his deep appreciation of Scotland's history and Gaelic heritage. Nothing could exemplify these points better than *The Immortal Isles*, his beautiful book about the Outer Hebrides. Take any few pages at random and you will find a fascinating mixture of sensitive, romantic descriptions of the islands and their beautiful skies, seas, and light, local place names and their meanings, legends and local customs, fine accounts on the flowers, birds, and seals, enthusiastic stories about his camping trips to photograph uncommon nesting birds from hides, and a reverence for the local people.

The book is also deeply interesting as it describes houses, customs and other aspects of the Outer Hebrides people in the early part of the 20th century. This way of life has since changed there faster than elsewhere in Scotland, and so Seton Gordon's book is a valuable record. When you go to the Outer Hebrides as a modern tourist, you will find it fascinating to visit the many places that are described in *The Immortal Isles*, and see how greatly they have changed in the last half century. You will also realise that the Gaelic culture is still alive, and indeed has a new breath of life. In *The Immortal Isles*, Seton Gordon, who worried that Gaelic would die, wrote "even in the Isles the iorram or rowing song is fast dying out, nor are the spinning, the reaping, and other songs of labour often heard, so that all lovers of things of the past should do their utmost to keep alive the old songs, the old traditions, the old language, of the Immortal Isles". He would have been glad to see that in 1979 the local government council in the Outer Isles is called Comhairle nan

Eilean, with a strong bi-lingual policy, and that
national policies for Gaelic have been taken up
by major political parties in Scotland.

Seton Gordon was a masterly describer of an
incident or event, and often did this so well that
for a moment the reader was there with him.
Here is an example from *The Immortal Isles*,
"Before we set sail on the return journey to Uist
we sat down to a wonderful tea: drop scones,
newly made and light as a feather, freshly
churned butter with the scent of the flowers of
the machair in it, and the richest of sweet
cream". Or a description of an evening at a
summer shieling, "After supper there was much
piping and dancing on the rough moorland outside, and as the moon rose golden in the east
there was the singing of old Gaelic songs, such
as Crodh Chailein and Fhir a' Bhata." Or the
last paragraph of the book, "During the month
one heard often the wild elusive call of a
wandering greenshank. Sometimes he fluted
beside some hill tarn; sometimes one disturbed
him at his feeding on the ooze beside a sea-pool
at low tide. There are few bird-calls more
wonderful than the cry of the greenshank. In
his voice the spirit of the wild places lives: his

love-song, heard at an immense height above some lonely Highland pine forest in spring, is deathless music that remains in the mind of him who hears it so long as memory lasts."

I am delighted that Seton Gordon's work will increase and live on afresh with this, the first reprint after his death. And I am glad that it is being published by a Scottish firm. A fresh spirit is about these days, a re-awakening of interest which fortunately goes far beyond party politics and which rekindles our distinctive culture and identity. The Outer Hebrides are a central part of this culture. I commend Melven Press for their pioneering spirit, and for their belief that classic excellence is timeless and never out of date. And I commend them for realising that any work which raises the spirit of man and brings him into closer communion with nature is of profound value. *The Immortal Isles* will delight present and future generations and be as immortal as the wonderful isles it describes.

Adam Watson
Crathes, 1979

THE IMMORTAL ISLES

INTRODUCTION

FIFTY miles west of the Scottish coast the Outer Hebrides rise from the Atlantic. Their ancient name was Innis Cat, and they are sometimes called Innis Fada or the Long Island, because from a distance the Isles seem to be joined one to another.

The Hebrides have had a romantic and turbulent history. In the year 888 King Harald of Norway added them to his Crown, and by the Norse the Long Island was ruled until 1265, when Magnus of Norway ceded all the Western Isles to Scotland.

One of the articles of this historic treaty provided that an annual sum should be paid by Scotland to Norway as compensation for that country's loss of the Isles.

Even to this day many of the place-names of the Outer Hebrides are Norse. Lewis, Harris, Uist, Bernera, Barra, Pabbay, Vatersay; all these names take us back to the time of the sea-roving Vikings. The most southerly of the Outer Hebrides is Barra Head (of which the old name is Bernera). From here, on a very clear day, the Irish coast may be seen on the southern horizon, and the rays of Barra Head Lighthouse have been observed from the Signal Station on Malin Head in Ireland.

If one sails on a northerly course up the Minch one passes in turn Barra Island—this must not be confused with Barra Head, as it is a number of miles north of the latter point —Eriskay (where Prince Charles Edward first landed on Scottish soil prior to the disastrous rising of 1745), South Uist (the ancient country of the MacDonalds of Clanranald), Benbecula (which may be reached from Uist at low tide across the South Ford), North Uist with its wild sea-caves, Harris of the great hills, and lastly Lewis, or, as it is sometimes named, The Lewes.

One spring morning I sailed north in a great liner that was making a special call at Lochboisdale in South Uist to embark a number of Isles folk who were emigrating to Canada.

An hour before sunrise we approached the most southerly of the Isles. In the serene sky a few clouds hung motionless, and as the sun climbed towards the horizon they glowed first crimson and then gold. Just north of where the rim of the sun was slowly rising stood Ben Cruachan of Argyll, its twin peaks, a full seventy miles distant, sharply silhouetted against the glowing horizon. Nearer at hand lay the Island of Mull—a magic isle set in a silent sea that seemed bespelled. Dominating that island was the great cone of Ben More, over 3000 feet high, and south of that hill the high cliffs of Lochbuie were clear-cut against the sunrise. South of the Isle of Mull rose the lonely lighthouse that is upon the highest point of the sunken reef known as Dubh Hirteach, and nearer at hand Skerryvore Lighthouse rose from a waste of waters, a needle-like object salmon-tinted by the rising sun. At the very moment of sunrise a solan goose passed the liner. Its keen eye noticed a great black-backed gull on the water eating a fish, and it swooped down and alighted on the sea. Here the sun reached only its head and neck, tinging them with crimson, while its body was in deep shade. The effect was very wonderful, and lasted for the space of a few seconds.

Off Mingulay, where great precipices give sanctuary to thousands of sea-birds, we passed many companies of guillemots, flying in little parties low over the surface of the water. Some of the birds were steering towards Mingulay, others were flying forth to distant fishing-grounds.

Soon the hills of South Uist showed ahead of us, and we sailed through a blue sunlit sea to drop anchor off Lochboisdale, where the air was heavy with sadness because so many of the people were leaving the island.

South Uist—of which Lochboisdale is the port —is an island rich in historical associations. Here Clanranald formerly lived with all the state befitting a Highland chieftain. Clanranald had his piper, his harper, his bard who sang the praises of his ancient house. The bardic order was preserved longer in Scotland than in any other country, for it was not until the year 1726 that the race became extinct. The last of all the bards, Neil MacVurich, was of distinguished ancestry. His forbears had for generations held the office of bard in the family of Clanranald, and for no less than fifteen generations had held the farm of Staoiligary and the four pennies of Drimisdale. The office of harper seems to have fallen into disuse about the same time as that of bard, for the last of the harpers, one Murdoch Mac-Donald, harper to MacLean of Coll, quitted his office in 1734.

It was in a lonely cave on the eastern shore of South Uist that Prince Charles Edward, after the " rising " of 1745 had ended in failure, hid for almost a month. Every islesman knew of his hiding-place, but not one was tempted into betraying the Prince, although the Government of the day offered a reward of no less than thirty thousand pounds for information concerning the hiding-place of the Royal fugitive.

Islands have always a certain fascination, but the spell of the Long Island is a peculiar one. Whence comes the indefinable charm that pervades the Outer Isles ? They are lonely, these isles, without shelter, treeless, the home of frequent storms and of mist-laden winds that sweep

across shores salt from the spray of the vast
Atlantic.   And yet to those who understand the
Isles how irresistibly do they call, so that one
who has sensed their serene, benign atmosphere
is drawn to them again and again, to gaze upon
the glorious sunsets, to watch the moonbeams
dance upon the great waves of the sea and upon
the lesser waves of the lochs, to hear the
musical clamour of the wild geese and the
mournful baying of the grey seals!

It is said that environment has a powerful
influence in moulding the character of us mor-
tals.   One would therefore expect to find in the
Outer Hebrides an unusually attractive race of
people; and one is not disappointed.   The people
of the Isles, in their simplicity, dignity, and
charm, are a race apart ; they have retained
to an unusual extent the natural refinement and
courtesy that distinguished the Highlander of
old.

Not long ago I entered a wee house where
an old lady lived by herself.   The house had no
chimney, and in the centre of the room a peat
fire burned, its smoke escaping through the
crannies in the thick walls (so that, from a
distance, one might have imagined the cottage

to be on fire), through the open door, and
through a hole in the roof. In the room the
blue peat smoke hung so thick that it was difficult at first to distinguish the old lady at her
spinning-wheel. Yet the room was spotlessly
clean, and the earth floor was sprinkled with
sand, carried up from the shore several miles
away with much labour.

To this old lady English was as much a foreign
language as, let us say, Russian is to the average
Briton. She had never left her island, and therefore, like many of the older people of the Isles,
had never seen a railway train. But she possessed
that indefinable charm and dignity which many
people well endowed with this world's goods
would have given half their wealth to acquire.

Because of the flower-decked machair-land[1]
and the sleepless Atlantic beyond, the western
shores of the Isles have a special charm. How
varied and altogether delightful is, for instance,
the western seaboard of North Uist. Here
sandy beaches alternate with rocky headlands.
Here the Atlantic rollers break in a smother
of spray that carries to the seaweed-built ravens'

---

[1] Machair = level grazing-lands on the Atlantic seaboard of
the Isles.

nests set precariously upon ledges of slippery rock where tufts of sea-thrift cling. How enormous are the waves which dash against Haskeir's northern cliff and, hurrying onwards, break upon Houghary Point, or spout high in a thin column through the small opening of a sea-cave known as Slochd a' Choire!

Haskeir [1] must be one of the most lonely of British Isles, and years may pass without a human foot treading its slippery rocky shores. In summer great numbers of sea-fowl nest here, and in winter the far-travelled clan of the barnacle geese feed upon its grassy crown.

It is said that, long ago, a man of the name of MacCrimmon, being desirous to meditate in seclusion upon the mysteries of life, prevailed upon the fishermen of Houghary to land him upon Haskeir. At last a day came when the Atlantic was sufficiently smooth for the voyage to be undertaken, and MacCrimmon was landed on Haskeir with a supply of food to last him through the winter months. There is a well

[1] Haskeir must not be confused with Heisgeir of the Monach Isles, or the Heiskeir of the Minch, where a lighthouse stands. In Blaeu's *Atlas* (1654) Haskeir is marked as being inhabited, but it must have been deserted soon after that date.

upon the island, so that he did not lack drinking-water. The season was autumn, and the fishermen promised to call for him next spring. Tradition is silent as to what befell this courageous man, but to this day are to be seen the ruins of a rough dwelling known as the Walls of MacCrimmon.

It is possible that this MacCrimmon was one of the line of the hereditary pipers to MacLeod. And, this being so, he would no doubt have composed masterpieces of *piobaireachd* or *ceol mor*, for he would have heard and understood the music of the sea, the clamour of the geese by moonlight, the ghostly cries of the petrels, the mournful calling of the grey seals at ebb-tide.

Haskeir is a Norse word, meaning Deep-sea Skerry, and one can picture the Norsemen of a thousand years ago sailing out to that lonely island after seals, or returning to North Uist through turbulent seas after a raid upon the sea-fowl and their eggs. But the Celt is a less daring mariner than the Norseman, and so Haskeir is now in solitude.

The sea music is present throughout the Isles. Thus the people themselves could not be otherwise than musical, and there are to be heard on

Innis Fada old Gaelic songs that have been lost
—if ever they existed—on the mainland.

But even in the Isles the *iorram* or rowing
song is fast dying out, nor are the spinning, the
reaping, and other songs of labour often heard,
so that all lovers of things of the past should do
their utmost to keep alive the old songs, the old
traditions, the old language, of the Immortal Isles.

THE GREY WIND

" From the East comes the Crimson Wind,
  From the South the White,
  From the North the Black,
  From the West the Grey Wind."

Seanchus Mor.

FAR beneath the western horizon, beyond the
lonely island group of Saint Kilda, beyond even
the surf-encircled cone of Rockall, is the magic
isle by name Flaith-innis.

One may visualise it when the setting sun dips,
a ball of glowing fire, below the Atlantic, when
distant Saint Kilda on the far horizon seems a
fairy island, and when the benign Spirit of the
West permeates both land and sea.

How interesting it is that the spiritual insight
of the Celt should have placed the three abodes
of the happy to the west of the last outpost of
land ! Flaith-innis lay west, and on that fairy isle

was the abode of perpetual youth, perpetual life, and perpetual love.   Westward, too, lay Tir nan Og, the Country of the Young, and Tir fo Thuinn, that mystic land set in Atlantic depths where many wonderful spiritual beings dwelt in joy on the ocean floor that stretched radiant away and away in the light of an eternal day.

And since the Grey Wind came from the west, there was held to be in it some peculiar occult essence.

Few can visualise the enchanted isles in these busy, materialistic days, and few even of those who have the visions care to talk about them ; but from the west, and perhaps upon the west wind, was said to come the Sluagh or spirit-host that was sometimes seen in the Isles.

I take the following arresting description of the Sluagh from *Carmina Gadelica*, a rare and little-known work containing an unrivalled store of knowledge on the spiritual history of the Gael : " On the Island of Benbecula two men were tending calves one night in a building known as An Tigh Fada, or the Long House. The men were sitting together talking beside the peat fire, when suddenly two strange dogs rushed into the room.   They sped round the house, to the terror of the calves and the dismay of the men. The dogs were leashed together on a leash of silver bespangled with gold and brilliant stones, which sparkled in the bright moonbeams and the flickering glow of the peats. Suddenly from the air without the house a voice was heard calling :

   " ' Sitheach-seang, sitheach-seang,
     Siubhal bheann, siubhal bheann,
     Dubh sith, dubh sith,
     Cuile rath, cuile rath,
     Cu gorm, cu gorm,
     Sireadh-thall, sireadh-thall.'

   " ' Slender fay, slender fay,
     Mountain traveller, mountain traveller,
     Black fairy, black fairy,
     Lucky treasure, lucky treasure,
     Greyhound, greyhound,
     Seek beyond, seek beyond.'

" The dogs, thus recalled, rushed out, and the men stumbled out after them. And there, in the velvet, moonlit sky, they beheld an innumerable host of spirits with hounds on leash and hawks on hand. The air was filled with music like the tinkling of countless silver bells, mingled with the voices of the Sluagh or spirit-multitude calling on their hounds.

" Then the numerous aerial company departed westwards, away and away toward Tir fo Thuinn and Tir nan Og beneath the great western ocean horizon.   Fortune follow them, and luck of game—and, oh, King of the Sun and the Moon and the bright effulgent Stars ! it was they who put fear and terror, and more than enough, on the men and calves of ClanRanald."

The Grey Wind is a wind of sadness, a wind of mystery.   It brings innumerable armies of mist from the limitless ocean, over which the tiny stormy petrel drifts like a lost spirit—mist so close and impenetrable that the solans from distant Saint Kilda are baffled and unable to take their bearings, and must needs sweep close into the shores of Uist on their passage to their east-lying fishing-grounds.   It brings soft sighings to the shores, soft sighings to the hazel woods that grow on some of the more sheltered Inner Isles.

The Grey Wind throws her veil over the moorlands and they are lost to view, and when rain—soft, kindly rain—accompanies, as it often does, the wind, the moors are a country of sound.

There is the murmur from innumerable, in-visible burns here, each burn a raging torrent of peat-stained waters which dash furiously onward, in a succession of waterfalls and deep yeasty pools, to the mother ocean, even as a soul, its life-journey over, joins itself to the unseen and infinite.

One September day I recall when the Grey Wind was the bearer of white drifting mists of unusual density. I was abroad on the open moorlands on this day, and walked through a dim and ghostly world. Occasionally overhead the mist momentarily thinned, and one saw the dim orb of the sun shine wanly upon the heather that was still rich in colour although the season of its flowering was almost at an end. Every ditch was overflowing ; every burn was a torrent ; every heather stem and blade of grass was saturated with moisture. And there seemed to brood on this day a spirit of sadness—that sadness which uplifts rather than depresses, and is peculiar to the sea-pervaded shores of the Isles.

Who has not crossed to the Outer Isles from the western mainland on a day when the Grey or the West Wind has been blowing, and as he crossed the Minch felt the spell of western seas ? How silently do the fulmar petrels glide on such a day ! For a moment only they are seen, sailing on wings which seem held always so stiffly, so rigidly, and then, almost before the eye has realised their presence, they are gone, steering an unerring course through mist-held aerial seas. How wild the scream of an Arctic skua on a day such as this ; how dark its swift-flying form that seems always to cleave the air with almost super-natural strength !

Should the Grey Wind advance with its silent mists at the season of autumn, how hazardous is the journeying of the migrating bird-people which steer southward above perilous seas at that time ! These bird-travellers lack the unerring sense of direction which the fulmars and some other sea-birds possess, and on dark misty nights countless thousands must find a watery grave.

I shall always remember the account which one of the lightkeepers at the lonely rock-station of Skerryvore gave me of the destruction caused by the lantern to the migrating bird-armies one autumn night when the Grey Wind was abroad. On such a misty night birds travel low, and the lantern rays have an irresistible and fatal attraction for the travellers. They press in upon it in clouds, striving to reach the fierce ray that, like some fierce sun-spirit, draws them to itself with compelling strength. Many birds that night struck the lantern and fell wounded to the rock below. Many more glanced off the smooth glass and perished in the sea—if indeed they were not dead when they reached the grey, heaving waters. The majority of the birds that night were fieldfares. These field travellers—for such is a translation of their name—had voyaged from the birch forests of Norway, like the Vikings who subdued the Western Isles of old, and were doubtless making for the Irish coast. Many, many of them fell, and the darkness resounded with their cries of alarm, wonder, and excitement as, too late, they attempted to save themselves from striking that deadly transparent wall of glass.

But in spring and early summer the Grey Wind comes seldom. Rather it is the Crimson Wind from the east, or the Black Wind from the north, that drifts across the Isles, bringing with it blue skies, and crisp, exhilarating air, so that the breeze is laden with the scents of innumerable growing things. The Black Wind, travelling down to the Isles from the frozen seas that approach the Pole, sweeps away the mists and the haze, so that distant hills seem near, and the jagged, snow-flecked spires of the Cuillin rise sharply into a fairylike horizon.

But although the Grey Wind may slumber long, the day will come, sooner or later, when once again it will advance from the west, will obscure the blue skies and each hill, high and low, and with its soft moisture will refresh the land.

THE RAVEN : A BIRD OF THE ISLES

"Tha fios fhithich aige." "He has raven's knowledge." "Piob mhor air an fhitheach." "The bagpipe on the raven" (that is, an impossibility).—*Old Gaelic Sayings.*

FOR several hundred years the Norse ruled the Isles, and thus in the Celtic west there has been through the centuries an intermingling of Norse sagas and Gaelic legends.

Since the raven was sacred to Odin, the principal deity of the Scandinavians—the Mars of Scandinavian mythology—it is only natural that the Lords of the Isles should have assumed the raven as their crest, because of their Norse descent through Ragnhildis, the wife of Somerled. In an illustrated manuscript called "Workman's," compiled about 1565, the arms of the Lord of the Isles are thus depicted : Or, an eagle displayed ; gules, surmounted by a galley ; in the dexter chief, a hand couped of the second ; crest, a raven proper, perched on a rock ; supporters, two bears, each pierced with an arrow.[1]

There is a tradition that the raven was the bird of the MacDougalls also, and Professor Watson tells me that Alexander MacDonald, the Gaelic poet, in his poem on a dove, calls the raven " dubhghall " (pronounced Dugall). The MacDougalls trace their descent from Dugall, Lord of Lorn and King of the Isles, who in the ninth century married a princess of Norway. Dugall, it is said, was the eldest son of Somerled, Thane or Regulus of Argyle, by his wife Ragnhildis, daughter of Olave Bitling, called Olave the Red, Norse King of Man and of the Isles.

When the Norse subdued the Isles, the Celtic natives doubtless heard much raven lore from the Vikings, who took with them always on their voyages of exploration a number of ravens, because of the power of these dark birds of sensing the direction of a land that was still invisible beneath the heaving horizon. Incidentally, it is said in the Norse sagas

[1] For this information I am indebted to Captain A. R. MacDonald of Waternish.

that the raven was the means of the discovery of Iceland.

In the west the raven is at the present day the emblem of good luck with stalkers, because it appears when a deer is killed, and to hear the raven's croak when setting out on a day's stalking fills the hunter's heart with joy.

The raven (with the possible exception of the heron) is first of all the birds to nest in the Isles. There is a saying, " Nest at Candlemas, egg at Shrove-tide, bird at Easter ; if the raven has not these he has death."

In every district of Scotland, except the uninhabited sea-girt isles of the west, the raven's life is a hard one. Wherever there is game-preserving each keeper wages war against this black-plumaged bird, which is classed with the grey crow as " vermin," to be shot or poisoned whenever possible. " Give a dog a bad name and hang him " is a saying which applies to the unfortunate raven. The bird of Odin, sacred of old, now receives no mercy. The bitterness against the grey crow one can understand and sympathise with, because the hoodie is a thorough rascal, and takes heavy toll of the eggs and young of many birds.

But the raven is chiefly a carrion-eater, feeding upon any dead sheep lying out on the moor, and soaring silently along desolate shores after a storm to search for the large crabs and fish of various kinds that have been cast upon the beach by Atlantic rollers.

So wary has the raven become from much persecution, that only in the Outer Isles is there any hope of finding a raven's nest in an accessible spot.

Late one March I heard from the Isles that a nest had been found on a steep heathery slope beside a loch in an excellent position for photography, and at the end of April, when the young ravens had been hatched, my wife and I sailed across to the Outer Hebrides.

A bitter wind from the north was bringing blinding snow-showers across the Minch. In Skye the ground was white almost to sea-level, and during the intervals between the squalls the high hills seemed to sleep beneath their mantle of snow. A skein of wild geese passed us flying north. They made slow progress against the wind ; it seemed strange that on a day such as this they should be steering northward to the icy shores of Greenland, or perhaps Spitsbergen, where they nest. This way and that the feathered company swerved as the gusts caught them, and at times a fiercer squall than usual seemed to bring them almost to a standstill. That evening the Outer Isles were covered with a snowfall heavier than any during the winter, but early next morning the sky was blue and the sun was pouring down its warm rays upon the treeless country of the Isles.

As we crossed a great stretch of boggy moorland to the ravens' nesting-place, each loch shone in the sun-flood and, except here and there upon the hills, no snow remained from the storm of the previous day. Beside the track a pair of grey lag-geese were feeding, and were so tame that they did not take wing when we approached, but ran a short distance into the heather as farmyard geese might have done. As we neared the ravens' nesting-site both birds flew agitatedly high overhead, calling repeatedly with their deep, far-carrying bark. A few days before, the keeper had seen one of the pair swoop down from a great height upon a greater black-backed gull which had unwittingly trespassed near the nest, and attack it so furiously that it fled shrieking in terror.

The ravens' nest was built on a little terrace some fifteen feet above the waters of a quiet moorland loch. It was protected from the rain (the raven is particular that its young shall remain dry) by very long heather that grew immediately above the nest and drooped over it, acting as a roof. In the nest were four half-fledged young, which crouched, silent and afraid, in their home as we neared it.

The hiding-tent was put up fifteen feet from the nest, and was covered over carefully with long heather so that not a square inch of canvas showed. But the ravens were suspicious, and three hours' watching in a bitter wind gave no success. This was only to be expected, as the raven is one of the most wary and intelligent of British birds, so next morning we again visited the nest hoping for better fortune. The bitter wind had died away. In the still air the sun's rays were pleasantly warm, and hill, sea, and the sister isle to the south were bathed in the soft, mysterious light of the west. As we approached the ravens' nest we could see three red-throated divers courting on the loch: with curious cries they dived, splashed their wings on the water, and spoke to one another in strange, harsh voices. One of the ravens was hunting afield; the other flew backwards and forwards, occasionally somersaulting two or three times in rapid succession in true raven fashion.

My wife was left to take the watch in the "hide," and the keeper and I walked ostentatiously away in order to distract the attention of the ravens. The watcher remained in her uncomfortable position from 10.30 until 5, and an hour and a half after taking up her "watch" had the satisfaction of seeing one of the ravens alight on the edge of the nest after much hesitation and anxious croaking. A little later both birds alighted at the nest, but only for an instant. Altogether during the six hours' "watch" nine visits were made, and one young one was fed by regurgitation at each visit. The young ravens were feathered, and during the intervals between meals they preened their feathers, amused themselves by pulling at heather stalks, and dozed frequently. But at the approach of either of their parents they became consumed by excitement. The following day I took the "watch." A strong southerly breeze was ruffling the waters of the loch, but on the steep heathery slope beside the nest there was shelter from the wind. A few minutes after I had been left in the "hide" a heavy shower passed over, and in the clear interval that followed the young ravens walked out of the nest and stood on the terrace, shaking the rain from their plumage and preening their feathers with the oil which they obtained from the gland at the base of the tail.

I had been in the "hide" just under an hour when a dark form flew low across the loch and one of the old ravens alighted at the nest. As she did so the brood croaked deafeningly in unison, and the parent with deeper cry added to the babel of sound. Rapidly she fed one of her family, inserting her bill and half of her head down the gaping mouth of the expectant fledgling. Having fed her child the old raven croaked frightfully, eyeing the lens of the camera with great suspicion before flying away. Five minutes later she, or perhaps her mate, returned and fed another of the clamouring brood. Altogether there were four visits within twenty minutes, but during the next two hours the ravens did not once appear, and

I had ample opportunity of watching the young-sters. One of the brood was indifferently grown and was a very depressed young person. He lay always in the cup of the nest and held his mouth open feebly, as though mutely asking for the food his more virile sisters and brothers almost always deprived him of ; for when either of the parents arrived, the rest of the brood trampled upon his prostrate form and concealed him from view.

Sometimes black-throated divers flew, croaking, above the " hide," and once the calls of wild geese were heard. Upon the loch red-throated divers and red-breasted mergansers swam, and a twite or mountain linnet made cheery music.

The next day the "watch" was taken by my wife, and she saw, through a tiny peep-hole in the side of the " hide," the courting of a pair of red-throated divers on the loch. During the courtship display the male diver as he swam repeatedly flapped his wings, which were bent close to his flanks. Occasionally he darted forward with his neck outstretched and parallel to the water's surface, so that he seemed curiously snake-like. Sometimes he dived in the midst of his flapping, and when at

a little distance from his approving mate he
uttered a cry very like a cat's "mee-ow."

Five days later, when next I took my watch
in the "hide," it seemed as though full summer
had come to the Isles. There was of old a Celtic
belief that the secret name for the month of
May was Love. And every lover of the Isles
knows that on a still, clear day in May there
is abroad a spiritual essence that uplifts the
heart and brings the spirit nearer to the realm
of the intangible. On the dark blue waters of
the many lochs the sunlight was sparkling ;
before the soft breeze the long heather bowed
gracefully. In the soft, mysterious skies a few
grey billowy clouds seemed to float motionless.
How immense do the skies always seem in the
Outer Isles where the horizons are limitless and
stretch from the ocean in the east to the ocean
in the west !

The ravens were becoming gradually accustomed to the hiding-tent and the camera lens
that stared unwinkingly at them, and this morning one of the old birds returned to feed the
brood less than half an hour after I had been
shut into the "hide." Four times in rapid succession she flew in across the loch and quickly

fed the young, and then, just before eleven o'clock, she finished her feeding and set out across the moorland to search for more food.

The young ravens were cheerful and very lively, for they caught the spirit of this glorious morning. They stood and flapped their wings with an excess of vigour, clinging tightly to the edge of the nest as they did so. At times they pecked playfully at the heather stalks of which the nest was made. An hour before noon they lay down in the nest and slept, but twenty-five minutes later were unexpectedly awakened by the arrival of their mother, and immediately there was intense excitement and much flapping of black wings at the prospect of ever-welcome food! Three times in quick succession the parent raven alighted on the edge of the nest, and each time she fed one member of the family. She did not seem to discriminate, but shoved the food down the throat of that child which, by its shrieking and general aggressiveness, made itself the most important personage. During these visits her throat was distended pouchlike with food, and once I saw her disgorge a piece of red flesh—perhaps a fragment from the carcase of some sheep.

In the early afternoon, as my wife and I were "changing over," both ravens flew in from the west, and hopped about on the grass on the opposite side of the narrow loch, the cock apparently feeding the hen.

Near the ravens' loch a pair of grey crows were nesting. The hoodie is much later to build than the raven, and this particular pair had not yet hatched out their eggs. On leaving the "hide" I saw what I imagined to be the male hoodie alight on some boggy ground and pull up carefully the long, withered coarse grass that grows amongst the heather in wet areas. Amongst the roots he must have found some worm or edible grub, and after a time he took wing in the direction of his sitting mate, meaning, I have no doubt, to feed her on the nest.

Across the calm waters of the Minch one saw the tempest-scarred peaks of the distant Cuillin, grey mists clinging to their slopes ; northward rose the heights of Harris. And from a great distance came the soft cadences of a wandering cuckoo—the "Returning One," as she is named in an old saga—that comes with the green wind and goes with the grey wind.

LOCH A' MHACHAIR

ALONG the western seaboard of South Uist many lochs lie. To some of them the spring tides penetrate, winding sinuously through hollows in the green machair, so that the waters of these lochs for days on end may be brackish, and the bladder wrack may float in long yellow lines upon the peat-stained surface.

But most of the lochs are out of reach of the long pulsating fingers of the Atlantic. Many of them, it is true, are only a few feet above sea-level at flood-tide, and at some future age will be one with the boundless ocean that is imperceptibly encroaching upon the land, so that in ancient villages the fronds of the sea-tangles wave, and over old burying-places great lythe and congers swim, and there is the green twilight of ocean depths.

Loch a' Mhachair is the Loch of the Machair that extends from one end of Uist to the other along the western margin of the Isle.   In summer this machair is a fairyland of flowers, but in winter and spring bitter winds sweep across it, and there is no tree, no bush nor shrub, to give shelter.

There is an old Gaelic saying, " Fast goes the man of the thriftless wife along the machair of Uist " ; for it is inferred that the clothes of that man are in bad repair, and thus the keen wind puts swiftness upon him, for it blows on him through his threadbare covering.

During most of the year the winds breathe uninterruptedly upon the waters of Loch a' Mhachair ; an army of waves or wavelets, according to the force of the wind, hurry across its shallow waters and break noisily on its leeward shore.

From the latter days of October until April the clan of the wild swans is rarely absent from the loch.

On days of tempest and when driving rains from the south-west cast their grey lances slantwise into the wind-torn waters, the swans majestically ride out the storm.   When frost is likely to bind the waters of the loch, the swans swim backwards and forwards day and night without a pause in their efforts to keep open a lane of water. They are said even to rise upon the water and beat the young ice with their wings. And all the while the restless white company call one to another, so that the quiet air is filled with a murmur of many musical, far-carrying voices.

A beautiful Gaelic "rune" was composed by a woman of the Isles on a wild swan which she had found injured and carried home. As the condition of the swan improved so did the condition of her sick child, and the woman, convinced that the swan was mysteriously helping her, composed many charming verses on the feathered guest.

In the Outer Isles it was of good omen to hear the wild swans in the morning before one's fast had been broken, especially of a Tuesday morning. It was also believed that to see seven, or a multiple of seven, swans on the wing ensured peace and prosperity for seven, or a multiple of seven, years.

In the Isles linger many legends concerning the wild swans. They are sometimes said to

3

be Norse princesses imprisoned beneath a spell.
Another tradition relates that they are ill-used
religious ladies under enchantment, who have
been driven from their homes and compelled
ever to wander and to dwell where most kindly
treated and where least molested.

Thus it is said to be most unlucky to kill
a wild swan.

There is a Gaelic rhyme—

> "Chuala mi guth binn nan eala
> Ann an dealachadh nan trath
> Glugalaich air sgiathaibh siubhalach
> Cur nan cura dhiubh gu h-ard."

> "I heard the sweet voice of the swans
> At the parting of night and day,
> Gurgling on the wings of travelling,
> Pouring forth their strength on high." [1]

How inspiring it is to see the wild swans in
a white compact company beating into the very
teeth of the storm that rushes across the machair
of Uist! With remarkable power of flight they
seem to slide, rather than fly, through the air;
upon them the gale has little effect, although its
strength is so great that even the gulls are forced
to take shelter. On these days of winter storm

[1] From *Carmina Gadelica*, by the late Alexander Carmichael,

the flying "scud" sweeps low across Loch a'
Mhachair, and wraps closely the corries of Hecla,
so that the cone of this grim hill is a country
of swift-driven vapours that sweep on impetuous
course from the vast spaces of the Atlantic to
the grim pinnacles and rocky aerial spires of the
Black Cuillin of Skye.

Beside the sleepless Atlantic there is life, even
in the depths of winter, and it is one of the
charms of the misty Isles that bird-life is almost
as plentiful at midwinter as during the long
serene days of June.

Beside Loch a' Mhachair is a winter haunt of
the barnacle goose, which has its summer home
so far into the Arctic regions that curious myths
persist concerning its reproduction.

In the Isles it is still believed by some of
the old people that the barnacle goose has its
birth from a barnacle, floating perhaps hundreds
of miles from land.   Another belief is that the
gosling falls from a barnacle that grows on a
certain tree found only on the Orkney Isles, on
one particular shore of that island group.   It is
in keeping with their mysterious origin that
the barnacle geese should arrive mysteriously at
their winter haunts beside Loch a' Mhachair.

One morning of late October a great company of
geese may be seen where the evening before had
been a waste of brown grasses, salt-encrusted and
lonely.   The geese stand there, a silent and alert
company, facing the wind.   After a time they
commence to feed on the grass which forms
their winter food ; but they are full of suspicions,
for they are in a strange land and know not
where an enemy may lurk.

Perhaps twenty-four hours earlier that silent
assembly had stood on the coast of Greenland,
or on the shores of hill-set Spitsbergen.   The
winter night was approaching.   Now for only
a few minutes at noontide could the pale sun
top those icy spires which rise so steeply from
the Polar sea that the winter's snow can find
no lodgment upon them.   Near the shore the
opaque emerald waters were already imprisoned
beneath the ice.

As the barnacle geese stood there, the impulse
of southern migration seized them.   Into the
frosty twilight they rose with musical clamour,
swung round several times, circling higher and
ever higher, then gathered themselves together
into their accustomed formation and headed south
towards the distant Hebrides that lay, remote

and invisible, fifteen hundred miles below the
southern horizon. It has been scientifically
established that wild geese on migration travel at
almost incredible speed, for in a goose that was
shot in Britain was found a shellfish, still un-
digested, which is known only in Polar seas.

The wild geese are more restless than their
cousins the wild swans, and although they pass
many winter days beside Loch a' Mhachair, they
fly often along the western shores of Uist, and
cross to the grassy uninhabited isles of the Sound
of Barra.

Other bird-visitors have their home beside
Loch a' Mhachair of Uist. Great flocks of
golden plover swerve and wheel in swift flight
above its low grassy shores, and grey-lag geese
often feed here. And upon the waters of the
loch are to be seen a great assembly of wild
duck of many different species.

There is an old tradition in the Isles that
when Christ in His wanderings was seeking to
escape from His enemies, He came to a wee croft
beside the Atlantic. He spoke to the goodman
of the house of His plight, and the crofter covered
Him over with his corn so that He lay concealed.
There were ducks on the croft, and when they

saw the sheaves temptingly spread upon the ground, they hurried up and fed eagerly upon the grain, but did not attempt to displace the shelter. But it was otherwise with the hens of that croft. When they in their turn found the corn and commenced to feed, they scratched and scraped until the Christ lay exposed. And as a punishment for this disservice the hens were no longer permitted to love the rain (as they had done previously) and the water, and from then onwards were in terror at the approach of a thunderstorm. But the ducks were still happy on the water and during times of rain, and with joy heard the oncoming thunder. And it is said to this day that when the duck hears the thunder she dances to her own Port a' Bial (mouth music).

In February the sun strengthens beside Loch a' Mhachair. In sheltered nooks the flower of Saint Bride of the Kindly Shores—the lowly dandelion — opens its orange-tinted florets. High above the loch float the ravens that, more than any other bird, feel the approach of spring. The raven was the sacred bird of the Norsemen of old, and at least one Highland clan—the Mac-Dougalls—have the raven to-day as their emblem.

At the battle of Clontarff in 1014 the Raven
Banner of Battle was used by Sigurd Jarl in his
battle with the Irish.   There was a prophecy
that the banner would always bring victory to
its OWNER but death to its BEARER, and during
this battle every man who in turn raised the
banner fell mortally injured.   Seeing this, Sigurd
Jarl himself snatched up the banner, saying as he
did so, " 'Tis fitting the beggar himself should
bear his bag."

Immediately he fell, and with his fall ended
the Norse power in Ireland.

It is in March that the first of its winter
visitors leaves Loch a' Mhachair.   Then the wild
swans spread their strong snowy wings and, rising
into the clear air, set their course northward
towards their summer homes in the Arctic.
Until April, or even May, the wild geese linger,
for their nesting-grounds lie still farther north,
and the snow in those high latitudes is slow
to melt.   With May arrive summer bird-visitors
beside Loch a' Mhachair.   One sees many
dunlin—quaint little birds, in size rather less
than a snipe—and the clan of the terns or sea-
swallows, fresh from the sunlight of tropical seas.

And now the grasses become slowly green, and

on quiet sunny days heavy trout break the placid surface of the loch and suck down the drifting flies.

On a grassy isle of Loch a' Mhachair a great colony of black-headed gulls nest, and often drift in a restless white cloud above the sunny waters. From the Atlantic shore close by terns sail in to join them with delicate fairylike flight.

All through the long sunny days of June larks mount high into the blue fields of heaven, pouring forth a flood of song—for is not the lark Fosag Mhuire, Mary's own special linnet?

In those wonderful days when the skies are blue, the air still, and the Atlantic indigo in tone, the machair is green no longer; it is a dreamland of flowers. In the gentle breeze that drifts fitfully in from the ocean the crimson orchis sways, and great fields of bird's-foot trefoil seem to throw back the sun-flood on innumerable golden blossoms. Beside the blue waters of the loch the white " cannach," or cotton grass, bows gracefully when the sea-breeze blows, and here and there a family of harebells show mystic blue flower-heads amongst the grasses.

In drowsy July days, when the air is heavy with scent, when the Atlantic slumbers, and

the ocean swell that passes over it seems but the
rhythmic pulsations of a deep sleeper, the clan of
the ragwort raise their stems above the surrounding herbage and hold to the sun their large
golden flower-heads.   During nights of storm, so
it is said, beings of the spirit-world hide themselves behind the stalks of the ragwort, and find
shelter enough here.   The ragwort, the eye-
bright, and the field gentian are among the last
of the flowers of the machair of Uist to blossom,
and ere they have faded the fierce equinoctial
gales sweep in from the west and spread sad
destruction over that land of flowers.

THE HERDSMAN OF THE TIDE-RACE

In Gaelic the great northern diver is Bun a'
Bhuachaille, which in English is the Herdsman
of the Tide-race. The waves of a tide-race, or
the steep-crested seas formed when wind and tide
strive together, are known in Gaelic by the
word *bun*. A friend of mine from the Isle of
Mull, Mr Robert MacMorran of Treshnish,
who has given me the Gaelic name for this
diver, informs me that the fierce tide-race of
the Lady Rock between the Island of Mull
and the lesser Isle of Lismore was known
as Bun nam Biodag, for the waves here were
said to be as sharp and keen as a dirk. A
mile or two south of the Lady Rock the channel
is much wider and the waves less steep, but the
sweep of the Atlantic tides is still evident. The
tide-race here is called Bun Mhor Somhairle, or
the Tide-race of the Great Somerled. And
since the great northern diver is essentially a

dweller amongst the tide-races leading to the channels and sea-lochs of the west, the name Bun a' Bhuachaille is a singularly appropriate one.

It was believed by the people of the Western Isles that this diver grew through several stages before it reached maturity. For the first seven years of its life it was a *laireig* or dabchick. It then changed into a *sgarbh* or green cormorant, and thus passed the following seven years. At the age of fourteen it grew into a cormorant with white spots on the thighs, and was then called Ball-re-Bothan, meaning perhaps "Spot-belly." For seven more years it continued as "Spot-belly," and it was not until it was twenty-one years of age that it was transformed into a Bun a' Bhuachaille or great northern diver.

Of the great northern diver, Martin over two hundred years ago wrote as follows in his *Description of the Western Islands* :

"The sea fowl Bunivochil, or as some Seamen call it, Carara, and others Bishop, is as big as a Goose, of a brown Colour, and the inside of the Wings white, the Bill is long and broad, and it is footed like a Goose, it dives quicker than any

Fowl whatever, its very Fat. The Case of this Fowl being flea'd off with the Fat and a little Salt laid on to preserve it, and then applied to the Thigh-bone, where it must lie for some Weeks together, is an effectual remedy against the Sciatica, of which I saw two Instance. It is observed of Fire-arms that are rubb'd over (as the custom is here) with the Oyl or Fat of Sea-Fowls, that they contract rust much sooner than when done with the Fat of Land-Fowl."

Bun a' Bhuachaille is a winter visitor to the seas of the Western Isles, and in May moves northward to Iceland to nest. It is a large and heavy bird, and in its nesting plumage—which it assumes just before leaving us—it is extremely handsome. Its head and neck are black, glossed with green and purple, and at the base of the throat is a band of white, marked with vertical lines of black. Lower down, on each side of the neck, is a similar but much larger patch forming a half-collar. The back and wing coverts are black, the breast white, and the eye red. In length this diver is thirty inches—that is eight inches longer than the brent goose—and from this its size can be judged.

The great northern diver arrives on western

seas in mid-October, and is with us until May. But during all this time it never once sets foot upon our coasts, for it remains afloat day and night and rides out the fiercest gales, unheeding the crested waves that so often break over it in a smother of white spray. It is an expert fisherman, and I believe there is a record of one entangled in a net set at a depth of no less than 180 feet below the surface.

The other bird fishermen of the tide-races—cormorants, shags, and red-breasted mergansers—fly at intervals backwards and forwards across the water as they change their feeding-ground, but the great northern diver travels always by water, not by air, when seeking new fishing-banks. Indeed it is a very rare thing to see it in flight at any time, and the islesmen believe that it is incapable of rising from the water.

And yet this belief is devoid of foundation, for the northern diver can on occasion fly both high and fast, and it seems most unlikely that the long northward migration from the Hebrides to the nesting-lochs in Iceland and Greenland is undertaken by water and not by air.

Until recently the great northern diver was not known in the Spitsbergen archipelago, but in the summer of 1924 my friend Mr Niall Rankin for some days observed a pair frequenting a loch which held the only species of freshwater fish in Spitsbergen—the Arctic char.

At its winter haunts off our shores the great northern diver is not difficult to identify, for it is considerably larger than its cousins the black-throated diver and the red-throated diver. Nor should it be confused with the shag or the cormorant, for it rides on the water differently from these two fishermen, and, although it swims deep, it floats more buoyantly than either of them, and its neck when swimming is not so far outstretched.

Its movements on the water's surface are leisurely, although its speed beneath the surface is remarkable. On the Skerryvore rock, a lonely lighthouse station some twenty-five miles west of Mull, a great northern diver was left by the tide in a rock pool perhaps twenty feet long and three feet broad. When observed by the light-keeper the bird did not attempt to leave the pool, but travelled beneath the water (the pool was three or four feet deep) backwards and forwards from one end of the pool to another. Its speed was so great that the eye could scarcely detect it, but saw only a white streak rush backwards and forwards without pause.

Indeed this great diver seems to progress more rapidly when submerged than on the surface of the sea, and I have noticed that when the mate calls from a distance of a few hundred yards, it dives and travels to it beneath the surface, perhaps emerging to draw breath on the way.

In the opening days of April the great northern divers begin to assume the nesting plumage. On the 1st of April I had five divers under observation at the mouth of a western sea-loch, and only two of them had commenced to grow their summer dress. Twelve days later a Bun a' Bhuachaille in full breeding plumage was fishing close inshore, and from its tameness I imagined it a passing migrant. On the twenty-fifth of the month two of the divers were courting, and during the late April mornings the birds were seen pursuing each other just after sunrise.

As late as 20th May one or two of the divers still lingered at their winter quarters ; the remainder had moved northward unobserved, and then one day the last of the winter visitors had left and the tide-race was deserted.

I imagine that the great northern diver is

able to remain submerged longer than any other British bird, but the duration of its dive depends largely on the depth of water in which it is fishing. I have timed many of these birds fishing at different depths. On 30th April a bird was fishing in shallow water. Its first dive lasted forty-two seconds, its second sixty-three seconds, its third forty-seven seconds, its fourth sixty seconds, and its fifth forty-nine seconds.

On 6th May two great northern divers were timed. One was fishing in deep water with a strong tidal stream ; the other was diving in shallow water where there was little current.

It will be seen from the following record that the dives of the deep-water diver were more prolonged. Its first dive lasted one minute seventeen seconds, its second exactly two minutes, its third one minute fifty seconds, and its fourth one minute thirty seconds. The dives of the bird working in shallower water were as under : First dive one minute twenty seconds, second dive fifty-two seconds, third dive fifty-three seconds, fourth dive one minute fifteen seconds.

On the following morning the waters were windless, so that the strong flood-tide could be seen like some live thing forcing its way inland.

The air was keen and virile, and on the hills a fresh coating of snow gleamed white. Upon the green waters three great northern divers swam lazily—a pair and an unattached bird. Although the divers were still hundreds of miles to the south of their nesting-lochs in Iceland or Greenland, the birds of the Isles about them were already nesting. On the shingle, above the mark of a high tide, handsome oyster-catchers were brooding their speckled eggs. The lap-wings had already hatched their chicks and wailed in alarm as they fluttered overhead. From the boggy ground redshanks called anxiously ; a wheatear darted from a rabbit-burrow where she was nesting. For some time I watched the solitary diver. The water where it was fishing was perhaps twenty-five feet deep, and the sea here was so calm that every movement of the fisherman could be observed. Unlike the shags and cormorants, which throw themselves half out of the water at the beginning of the dive, the great northern diver submerges with scarcely a ripple, driving itself downward with its powerful feet with no apparent effort. The diver must have been fishing for some time before my arrival, for after its fifth dive it remained on

4

the surface, preening its feathers and showing no inclination to return to its fishing. Between each of its dives this bird rested regularly for some twenty-five seconds.

A great northern diver when it is fishing is not an easy bird to keep under observation. A shag or a cormorant, an eider or a long-tailed duck, reappears more or less where it dived, but a great northern diver may travel several hundred yards beneath the surface, so that it is not easy to mark it immediately it emerges. It is a voracious feeder, and it is on record that one was choked by a grey gurnard which it had attempted to swallow.

I have frequently seen a great northern diver making desperate efforts to swallow a flounder. This flat fish—as may be imagined—is most difficult to dispose of, and it is curious that the diver always submerges if it has any difficulty with its "catch." Young coal-fish are caught by the divers in great numbers, but only one diver out of the many which I "timed" was seen to rise to the surface with a fish in its bill. It may be that only the more unwieldy fish are brought to the surface; certainly on this particular occasion the captive was hard to swallow, and at length the bird inadvertently dropped its "catch," immediately diving in pursuit, but apparently failing to recapture it.

During the day the herdsmen of the tide-races seldom sleep, but even when asleep the birds swim automatically, and keep their station unaffected by the wind and tide that ceaselessly play about the Hebridean Isles.

AN ISLAND MEMORIAL

I⊤ is late August, and the summer sun shines down on the Outer Hebridean isle of North Uist from a sky of azure.

Across the blue, serene plains of the Atlantic the south wind blows softly.

The blue of the sky is reflected from a multitude of moorland lochs; in the sunlight the waters flash as the wavelets lean to the sun.

There is a strange animation abroad upon the isle this August day. Along the narrow roads many people are making their way.

Men and women are dressed in the black clothes which they wear of a Sabbath, but here and there is seen the broad blue bonnet of a

Lovat Scout or the red tartan kilt of a Cameron Highlander. From all parts of the isle the people are converging on a little heather-clad knoll on which stands the memorial to the men of North Uist who gave their lives for Scotland and the Isles during the Great War. A Union Jack drapes the memorial; at noon it is to be unveiled by Lochiel, who has made the long journey from Achnacarry on the mainland to pay his last mark of respect to his late comrades in arms.

The little hill on which the memorial stands is less than a hundred feet above the sea, but from it one can see, this clear summer day, many, many hills, lochs, and isles. On the far-distant western horizon, faint and ethereal across ocean leagues, the Saint Kilda group of islands stands. At a lesser distance, and more southerly, the broad golden sands of the Monach Isles gleam in the sun's rays. Far to the south the hills of Barra (the Isle of Saint Barr) form the horizon; nearer at hand floating clouds rest lightly upon the big hills of South Uist. North stand the Harris heights; east is the island of Skye, the home of Cuchulain and other legendary heroes of the Gael.

Truly it is a fair scene on which the eye rests to-day, and one to fill the mind with joy. And yet in the hearts of the men and women who are journeying—slowly and with difficulty, some of them, for they are very old—to the little hill a great sorrow lies, for many sons of Uist went out to France and other zones where the Great War consumed human life, and few of them returned.

And yet happiness mingles, as it were, with the people's sorrow, for in their hearts they feel that all is well with their loved ones, since they went the only course that was open to them without sacrificing their manhood.

Towards midday a crowd gathers around the memorial. From the neighbouring Isles of Ballyshare, Grimsay, and Benbecula some of the people have journeyed, crossing the wide fords barefoot at ebb-tide. There are old men and women whose only speech is the homely Gaelic, girls and boys to whom the war is but a name. Many of the ex-Service men wear their medals.

The hour for the unveiling arrives, but the tide has not yet sufficiently receded to enable the people to cross the fords, and so the ceremony is postponed for half an hour.

The time passes quickly, and now the pipers

take up their position beside the memorial ; an air of sorrowful expectation pervades the silent assembly.

Lochiel, the chief of the Camerons, is greeted respectfully as he arrives on foot. The Lochiel of his day has ever been an honoured name in Highland history, and the present chief raised and commanded the 5th Battalion Cameron Highlanders.

There is a short pause, and then the slow, sad strains of a Gaelic psalm are heard. The singing commences haltingly, but with each verse gathers power, and at a little distance the sorrowful cadences are carried on the breeze like the murmuring of waves on a distant shore. Around the memorial are sad faces, singing brokenly with the memory of absent dear ones strong upon them.

Follows a Gaelic reading of Scripture by Doctor Donald MacDonald, the beloved parish minister of the isle, and then Lochiel, who has been introduced by Sir Arthur Campbell Orde, the Laird of North Uist, rises to address the people. His voice carries clearly across the hillside, with its purple heather on which peats are drying in the sun, and soon he is telling his eager listeners how he was asked by Lord Kitchener in the early days of the war whether he (Lochiel) could raise a battalion of the Cameron Highlanders. How successful he was is now history, but it is perhaps not generally known how heroically the battalion fought at Loos, and how many of its men fell there. Lochiel (although in his speech he does not mention it) escaped death on that occasion by a miracle, according to those who fought beside him.

As he speaks to the Isles folk Lochiel tells them that three emotions should be present in the minds of those assembled round the memorial— sorrow because of the loss of so many valuable lives, pride that their men should have met so noble an end, and resolution that their great example should be present ever in the minds of all.

The names of the fallen are now read out, and the pipers of the Scouts and Camerons play that touching lament, " The Flowers of the Forest."

On the heather, a little apart from the crowd, a man sits rocking his head in his hands in silent poignant grief ; as the pipes are silent, and as the strains of the Last Post drift across the moor, he is unable to control his lamentations and hurries away.   But near him children laugh and play—for to them the sorrowful memory of the Great War is a thing unknown — and dogs scamper around one another in light-hearted frolic.

The impressive ceremony is now at an end, and the people gradually disperse, after placing simple wreaths upon the memorial.   But many last lingering looks are directed towards it, and the single Gaelic word Cuimhneach, which in English is Remembrance, is read again and again.

Stern and enduring does the memorial stand, for it is of the granite of the hillside and surmounted by a Celtic cross.   It is built on consecrated ground, and twice a year the Sacrament is partaken of on this knoll, the worshippers leaving the church nearby to attend this solemn ceremony.

The sun still shines as the people " take the road " once again.   Some of the old folk are very tired, for they have already walked many miles, and their hearts are heavy.   Fair Saint Kilda has wrapped herself in a mantle of soft spiritual blue ; behind it towers a great bank of cumulus clouds.

They seem like lofty, incredibly distant peaks, and one feels that behind them, hidden from mortal eyes, lies Tir nan Og, the Country of the Blessed, and the home of those whose names have just been honoured upon this fair Hebridean isle.

THE GREY WIND BRINGS IN THE CRESTED WAVES

THE RAVEN'S POUCH BULGES WITH GOOD THINGS FOR THE FAMILY

THE RAVEN ALIGHTS TO FEED HER YOUNG

TWEED WEAVER'S HOME AT GEIRINISH, SOUTH UIST

OCTOBER ON THE MINCH

CROFTER'S HOUSE AND STEADING TYPICAL OF THE HEBRIDES

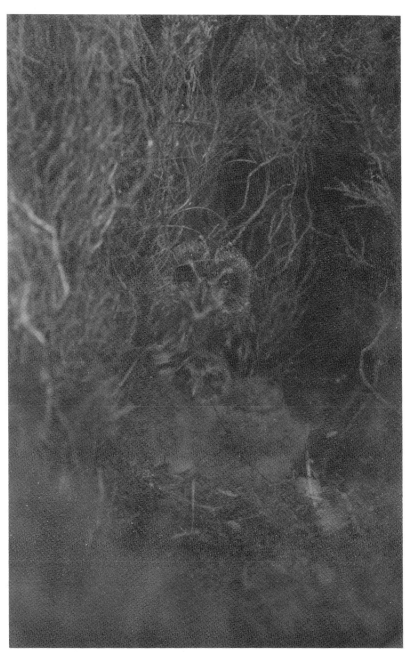

SHORT EARED OWL AT HOME WITH HER FAMILY

BLACK THROATED DIVERS ON THEIR NESTING LOCH

BLACK THROATED DIVER ON HER NEST

THE DIVER WARILY APPROACHES HER NEST

SPINNING ON THE OLD FASHIONED SPINNING WHEEL

THE WILY HOODIE AND HER SPOILT CHILD

ARCTIC SKUA SETTLING ON HER EGGS

A MERLIN ON HER NEST

USING THE OLD CAS CHROM OR FOOT PLOUGH

LAZY BEDS FOR GROWING POTATOES

HARROWING BY HAND

JUNE IN NORTH UIST

IT is June in North Uist as I write, and after weeks of cold, rough weather full summer has come swiftly from the south to the Long Island. The innumerable lochs lie tranquil, their peaty waters reflecting and intensifying the blue of the sky ; each island hill stands clear-cut against the horizon in the soft light of the far Western Isles.

It is only now that the crofters are finishing the sowing of their crop oats. A June sowing is a rare thing, even in the Isles, but the past spring was sunless, and the rains of April and May saturated the heavy peaty soil ; much of the June sowing cannot mature unless the summer be unusually fine.

But now the discomforts of spring are for-
gotten in the long days of glorious sunshine and
light breezes.   The soft wind blows in westward
from the Minch in the early morning, then gradually veers sunwise, and later in the afternoon
drifts in from the limitless Atlantic to the north-
west.

Even in this wonderful weather the Atlantic
is not silent ; the distant boom of the great
waves is carried across the lonely, deserted miles
of lochs and peat-bogs that form the interior
of North Uist.   At times ghostly fog-banks
lie to westward, above invisible and distant
waters, and the fog signal of some far-off lighthouse carries clearly through the still early
morning air.

All through the night herds of cattle pass
over the island.   The cattle sales are being held
in Barra, Benbecula, and North and South Uist,
and the beasts are being driven slowly along the
dry, dusty road from one island to another.   The
drovers talk animatedly amongst themselves in
the Gaelic.   They are fresh and cheerful at
midnight as at noon, for among the Isles-folk
night at midsummer is scarcely a time of sleep ;
most of them take their rest in the small hours,

when the sun after his short absence climbs once
more from the wave to shine upon the lochs, the
treeless hills, and the gently heaving ocean of the
western country.

How wonderful is a perfect day of midsummer
in the Isles! The horizons seem limitless. There
are no trees to shade the sun and the light is
brilliant. At sunrise the sky north-east burns
with soft rosy glow, and the pale moon hangs like
a sickle above the Minch, where countless puffins
and shearwaters fish, and the tribe of the herring,
king of fishes, plays. At noontide sea and land
seem to slumber in the intense heat. The deer
seek north-lying slopes, where there is some slight
shade, or lie in the bogs. In the cool of the
evening many birds are abroad, and great black-
backed gulls sail at an immense height, uttering
their hoarse, far-carrying bark. At twenty
minutes past ten (the people of the Isles do not
observe summer-time, and so the sun's setting
by their time is twenty minutes past nine) the
sun, hanging like a ball of fire upon the horizon,
seems, pulsating with life, to touch the sea. A
few minutes pass, and he is lost to view. But
even now Eaval and the other hills of North
Uist receive his soft rays ; then, at last, he is

gone, perhaps to shine a while on Tir nan Og, that spiritual land which lies beneath the western horizon.

And when the midsummer dusk, soft and pearly grey, broods upon the waters, the Blue Men (who with the Northern Lights and the Elves were cast from heaven long, long ago) play upon the Minch in mad, restless energy while their mortal cousins take their rest.

From the Outer Isles at sunset one may see a fleet of herring-drifters steam westward from Mallaig, their home port. Off Uist they cast overboard their long nets and lie beside them through the hours of dusk. Before sunrise they lift the nets, and the silvery living harvest which they contain, and set their course eastward for the Point of Sleat and Mallaig beyond it.

Upon Eaval of North Uist, the highest hill of the island, a pair of golden eagles formerly had their eyrie. One of the birds was shot a number of years ago, and since then the eyrie has been deserted. This pair of eagles did good, for they preyed largely upon the wild cats that are so numerous on the island and are so destructive to its grouse. These cats are not truly wild, for they are animals (or descendants of animals) which have been carried far into the moorlands by crofters who no longer wanted them but who were, perhaps, too kind-hearted to put an end to their former pets. These deserted favourites thrive and multiply on the rats and mice that are so plentiful in Uist, and do much harm to the ground-nesting birds.

Before the days of steamers North Uist received its mails and goods by sailing-packet from Dunvegan in the Isle of Skye, about twenty-five miles to the eastward, where in spring the shores of the lochs are golden with countless primroses. On swift wing solan geese make their way above the blue waters beside Dunvegan Castle, the ancestral home of the chiefs of the MacLeods. Here in past centuries the MacCrimmons, peerless among pipers, composed with much fasting and steadfast concentration these *piobaireachd* tunes of classical pipe music that are still played the world over.

In the days of the MacCrimmons North Uist was one of the lands of MacDonald of the Isles, South Uist the territory of Clanranald, Harris the country of MacLeod of Harris. Now all those old families have gone from the Isles which they once owned, but at Dunvegan the Mac-Leods remain, although not for a hundred years have the MacCrimmons made sweet music within the castle walls.

THE BLACK-THROATED DIVER

THE black-throated diver is one of the most handsome of all British birds, but it is so scarce and elusive that few people are familiar with its beauty.

Except during the nesting season the black-throated diver never comes to land. And when she nests she lays her eggs as near as possible to the water's edge, so that she may dive, seal-like, into the friendly depths on the approach of danger. The black-throated diver does not nest in England, nor in the lowlands of Scotland; but in the north-west Highlands it is found on many of the lochs. Its nesting habits are somewhat different from those of the red-throated diver. The red throat chooses a small tarn for its nesting-place, and does all its fishing in the sea, often a number of miles away. The black throat haunts larger lochs, and fishes in its own lake, and not in salt water.

There is one peculiarity of both divers while at their nesting haunts—they both dive from the nest into the water and will not readily take flight. Since the red throat's tarn is usually a very small one, the bird will, it is true, take wing and fly right away if it is disturbed too persistently. But the black-throated diver, having a larger sheet of water on which to swim, very rarely flies at all during the nesting season.

Early in April the black-throated divers arrive at their loch. They have passed the winter on the stormy sea, perhaps hundreds of miles to the south of their nesting quarters, and when they arrive at their summer home are in all the beauty of their nesting dress. The two large oval eggs are laid early in May. So close is the nest to the water that the eggs are sometimes washed away by a rise in the level of the loch.

This is the song that the black-throated diver sings in Gaelic when the loch is high and rising—

> " Mo chreach, mo chreach,
> M' eoin 's m' uibhean.
> Mo chreach, mo chreach,
> M' eoin 's mo m' uibhean.
> Mo dhith, mo dhith,
> Mo linn 's an tuilinn.

Mo dhith, mo dhith,
Mo linn 's an tuilinn.
M' urragan !
M' ulagan !
M' eoin !
M' uibhean !
M' ulaidh !
M' eislean ! " [1]

" My sorrow, my sorrow,
My chicks and my eggs.
My sorrow, my sorrow,
My chicks and my eggs.
My grief, my grief,
My brood in the flood.
My grief, my grief,
My brood in the flood.
My chicks !
My gifts !
My birds !
My eggs !
My treasures !
My troubles ! "

This is a very charming rhyme that in olden
times used to be repeated often by the people
of the Isles.   It will be seen that the composer
of these lines did not realise that the young divers
of all birds are the most fitted to stand a flood,

[1] From *Carmina Gadelica*, vol. ii. p. 313, by the late
Alexander Carmichael, LL.D.

for they are able to swim and dive with ease
and speed from the hour of their birth.

There was an old idea that in very dry
weather, when the waters of the loch were
shrinking, the divers became weak and restless.
And so when the loch-level is low the diver
sings—

> " Deoch, deoch, deoch,
>   An loch a traghadh.
>   Deoch, deoch, deoch,
>   An loch a traghadh.
>   Burn, burn, burn,
>   Mo luth 'm fhagail.
>   Burn, burn, burn,
>   Mo luth 'm fhagail." [1]

> " Drink, drink, drink,
>   The loch is drying.
>   Drink, drink, drink,
>   The loch is drying.
>   Water, water, water,
>   My strength is failing me.
>   Water, water, water,
>   My strength is failing me."

On a large grassy island of a loch of the west
a pair of black-throated divers nest each May.
The island is thronged with bird-life.   Here

[1] From *Carmina Gadelica*, by the late Alexander Carmichael,
LL.D.

nest in harmony herring and lesser black-backed gulls, oyster-catchers, dunlins, sandpipers, and a pair of fierce greater black-backed gulls.

One sunny morning of early June three of us—a friendly keeper, my wife, and I—rowed across to the island. Some time before we reached it the gulls rose in a drifting cloud into the clear air, but both divers swam around a few yards off-shore in a state of agitation. When we landed upon the island we found that the young divers had just hatched. Appearing like small balls of sooty down they lay in the nest, but, since their parents called them repeatedly and anxiously, one of them escaped to the water, which of course it had never entered before. Its skill in the water was a revelation. It swam out strongly and joined its parents, and, aided by a following breeze, in five minutes had covered fully three hundred yards. It swam between its parents, and when they dived it dived with them. The old divers were most anxious for the safety of their young. What we imagined to be the cock often uttered a loud yelp, rather like the howl of a dog. Sometimes, immediately after yelping, he made a great splash and then dived ; in order, no doubt, to distract attention from the young. The female sometimes uttered a wailing cry, and both parents seemed to call to the young with a soft grunting note.

Two days later we again rowed towards the divers' island. The sky was cloudless. The waters of the loch gleamed and sparkled in the hot midsummer air. The divers were swimming near the shore of the mainland, a few hundred yards from their nesting island. After a time they swam out towards that island, and then we could see that they had one of their chicks with them. Suddenly one of the lesser black-backs which was nesting on the island spied the baby diver and, flying out over the loch, swooped down upon it. The diver chick had just previously been having a ride on its mother's back, but, as ill-luck would have it, was some yards from her at that moment. A couple of seconds more and the gull would have carried away the chick, but, quick as thought, I shouted at the top of my voice, and our collie dog Dileas joining in the outcry, the gull swerved off, and the situation was saved for the moment. But the mother diver, mistaking our intentions and fearing we had designs on her chick, sprang out of the water with a wild cry and flew straight at the boat, passing within a few feet of it.

We headed the young diver carefully away from the danger zone, and kept it in view until it was beyond the territory of the marauding gull. And then, seeing all was well, we rowed quickly away from the spot.

We had given up the idea of attempting to photograph a black-throated diver on her nest for that season, when unexpectedly—for the nesting season was well advanced—we saw a black throat on a neighbouring loch swim ever closer to one of the islands, and at last clamber ashore and settle down on her eggs !

Unfortunately for us there was no boat on the loch, but we remembered the offer of a friend to lend us his collapsible canvas boat, and at once went over to his house about ten miles away.

The boat we transported so far in a car, then my wife and I dragged or carried it across a seemingly interminable bog. But when we attempted to inflate the bladders of the boat we found that, through age, the rubber was perished, and having no repair outfit with us, there was nothing for us to do but to launch the frail craft with the bladders empty. My wife, being the lighter of the two, made the first passage to the island. She took with her the camera and plates, and as she paddled across I paid out a long line, one end of which was tied to the boat, so that I might be able to pull the boat back and paddle myself across in my turn.

When loaded with passenger and camera the frail craft was less than an inch above the water-line. It was a work of art to sit down in it without capsizing the whole outfit. But at last my wife commenced her passage, with the camera poised on her knees and toes to keep it out of the water—for the craft leaked as well as shipping the water over the low sides. After some tense minutes she reached the island. When I had pulled the crazy boat half back, the dis-concerting discovery was made that the paddle remained upon the islet! Here was a pretty state of affairs. On the island was my wife, with no boat, only a paddle; here was I on the shore of the mainland with a boat, but no means with which to propel it, and no sticks to use as a paddle within thirty miles! The day was cold, and the prospect of swimming eighty yards and back again uninviting, not to say dangerous, as

anyone who knows the coldness of the water of
a Highland loch will believe.   But the crisis was
averted by our collie dog Dileas.   She is a
famous swimmer, and, being called by my wife,
swam across at once to the island.   There my
wife tied the paddle to her tail, carrying the
weight to the water's edge and pushing it off as
I whistled to Dileas from the mainland.   The
collie swam swiftly across the channel, towing
the paddle behind her.   She did not seem to be
aware of it until she was leaving the water,
when, feeling an invisible something pulling at
her from behind, she became filled with alarm, so
that I had difficulty in untying the knot round
her tail.

My own passage across was full of excitement;
several times I shipped so much water that I got
ready to swim for it, but somehow righted the
craft at the last moment.

A few yards from the diver's nest we built a
rough " hide " of stones and turfs, which we cut
with a spade that we had ferried over with us.
The diver all the time was swimming near.
Occasionally she stretched one wing and sometimes rose up on the water, flapping her
wings.   At times she swam with one foot only,

holding the other, paddle-like, away from her
side.

It was interesting to observe that she took
alarm from the alarm-cries of the gulls which
were also nesting on the island. She made a
delightful picture as she swam there, the feathers
on her back wonderfully barred with black and
white, her neck a beautiful ash-grey, and her
eye red.

Our return journey to the mainland was even
more precarious than our crossing had been. A
breeze had sprung up, and waves were chasing
each other down the narrow channel. The only
one to enjoy that crossing was Dileas, and she
swam disdainfully over, seeming contemptuously
surprised at the fuss we made over the simple
business.

Three days later we again crossed to the island.
In the meantime we had with much labour
repaired the damaged rubber of the two bladders,
so that now the craft floated higher on the water.
The black-throated diver did not realise we had
landed on her island. As we crossed the crown
of the islet we saw her for a moment sitting on
her eggs about twenty yards from us. Then,
like a seal, she sprang from the shore into the

loch with a magnificent noiseless dive, and continued beneath the water until she was well out into the loch.

We now quickly built up the "hide," and with camera in position I sat doubled up for the first watch, and my wife and Dileas hid themselves in the long rushes at the extreme end of the islet. The diver, swimming low and diving repeatedly as she approached, returned to the edge of the loch beside the nest within ten minutes, and was just about to land when she caught sight of the lens of the camera and sheered off.

When photographing birds near water the lens is a most difficult thing to conceal. It reflects the image of the water, and so seems to the bird almost luminous, and very alarming. For two hours the black-throated diver swam maddeningly backwards and forwards a few yards away. She was not really alarmed, but merely suspicious, and was unwilling to leave the element on which she was thoroughly at home for the uncharted land. All this time I dared not move lest any sound should increase her suspicions, although the desire to stretch my cramped limbs was almost overpowering.

During this time I saw one curious thing happen. On a larger island, perhaps a hundred yards away, was a colony of gulls. A greater black-backed gull crossed this island and picked up some small object, which I am sure was a young chick. It was flying off with its prize when it was set upon by the whole gull colony.

"Splendid birds," the reader may exclaim, "to protect their young so bravely!" Not a bit of it! The flock were all after the big gull, because they hoped to make it drop its prize, and then have a dash at it themselves, and try to swallow it before the mob set upon them in their turn. At last the great black-back, being thoroughly hustled, did drop its prize in the water. At once all the gulls swooped down upon it, and there was a fight, with wild cries, for the prize on the loch's surface, as though the prey were a shoal of fish on a sea-loch, and not one of their own young!

Time after time the diver was on the point of landing, and then, as I scarce breathed from intense anxiety, she deliberately turned about and swam gracefully a few yards out into the deeper water. No one who has watched a black-throated diver at such close quarters can fail to be impressed with the beauty of her plumage and the grace and power of her swimming. She gives the impression of possessing unlimited reserve strength, and swims just as easily against the wind as with it. She reminded me of a torpedo-boat destroyer as she suddenly, without effort, increased her speed in the teeth of a fresh breeze. By comparison with her the lightly floating gulls were as sailing craft. Sometimes as she swam she turned almost on her back and preened her beautiful flanks, that were as snowy as the plumage of a sea-gull.

At the end of two hours she seemed to make a sudden decision to seek out her mate and discover what he thought of the disturbing eye that was peering at the nest. She rose from the water—a very unusual thing for a black-throated diver to do at her nesting loch—and flew swiftly west into the teeth of the wind, calling once as she flew. I profited by her absence to leave the "hide," and we "set to" and built an archway of stones over the lens so that it was less conspicuous from the water. This done, I was again shut up in the small "hide."

Both black-throated divers were now swimming on the loch, the hen having evidently brought the cock back with her. Together they swam round the bay near the eggs. Perhaps owing to the moral support of her mate, perhaps because the lens did not now seem so formidable, the hen diver had more courage than before. She swam ever closer inshore, and at last, to my delight, shoved herself over the stones on her breast—for the divers are unable to walk upright—then climbed the bank, and at last settled herself upon her two beautifully marked eggs.

A HEBRIDEAN LEGEND

THE quietness of a Sabbath afternoon brooded over the Hebridean island of Benbecula.

The season was summer. From the green grazing-land adjoining the Atlantic ocean the scent of innumerable flowers was wafted upon the light sea-breeze. Clover and wild orchis, silverweed and bird's-foot trefoil, harebell and knapweed, held their flower-heads to the summer sun, and their perfume mingled with the salt smell of the ocean and the seaweed that lay piled up on its sandy shore.

From the blue vault of heaven larks sang. Ravens haunted the shore and, just beyond the line of breaking surf, solan geese winged their way towards distant Saint Kilda that rose faint and blue above the far north-west horizon.

Upon a lonely skerry an Atlantic seal had poised itself, and was occupied in resisting the efforts of the oncoming tide to wash it from its half-submerged resting-place.

Upon the machair an old Gaelic-speaking herdsman was tending a great herd of cattle. They were the property of all the crofters who lived in that part of the island, and were pastured daily in a great company. The herdsman had the land to himself, for, since it was Sunday, the people were remaining within their small thatched houses until the evening hour should call them to the Gaelic service in the wee church beside the shore.

The evening was a cloudless one. In the soft light the golden sands of the Monach Isles gleamed, and, after sunset, the lamp of the lonely lighthouse that warns vessels of the sunken reefs north of the Monachs was lit, and stabbed the velvet dusk. Then, one by one, the eternal lamps of the sky shone brightly through the cold abysses of limitless space.

As the last of the sunset burned dimly on the western horizon, and whimbrel and curlew made wild, mournful music above the shore, a furtive figure might have been seen to emerge from her small chimneyless cottage and, closely shawled, make her way across the machair towards the sandy beach.

Her errand was apparently an innocent one— to pull the roots of a certain plant from which is extracted a red dye. Why, then, the efforts of the woman to avoid observation, the stealth with which in the gloaming she sped silently across the machair?

The plant which gives the red dye is the yellow bedstraw. Its roots are so widely ramifying and deep-set that they hold the sand together, and without them much of the machair would be disintegrated by the fierce storms of winter. And so the gathering of the roots of this plant, known in the west as "rue," is forbidden by the islesmen.

The night wore on. In the southern sky the moon, a silvery orb, mounted serenely. A cold dew laid its moist hand upon the machair. The birds were silent, all save the ever-wakeful curlew and the oyster-catcher, Saint Bride's bird, who, it is said, once saved Christ from His enemies by covering the fugitive with seaweed as He lay exhausted upon the shore. The deep roar of distant surf upon some outlying reef carried far over the sleeping land.

6

Morning came, and larks mounted upon tireless wing high into the heavens in full-throated song. In the fields of growing barley the corncrake, the fairy bird of the Gael, called rhythmically.

The clachan of which the woman was an inmate bestirred itself. From the chimneys— or from the open door where the house was without a chimney—rose the blue smoke of peat fires. The men, their breakfast over, went to the fields to gather in the hay ; from the cottages shawled women emerged to milk the cows and feed the hens.

It was after midday when the absence of the woman was remarked upon. Her house was ominously quiet and deserted, but at first it was thought she had, perhaps, gone on a visit to a neighbour. That afternoon an organised search was made for her, and during subsequent days each unfrequented nook of the island was visited, without success.

The woman was never again seen in mortal form.

Not long afterwards the Teine Mor, or Big Fire, was first observed on the island. People whose business took them across boggy places after dark saw with apprehension a bright light flit restlessly hither and thither above the marshes.

Now this light had never been known on the isle previously, and when scarcely a night passed without its appearance, the idea gradually took form in the minds of the people that this was the restless spirit of the woman who had been taken, evidently, by the powers of darkness because of her wrong-doing. Of her fate many stories were whispered round the peat fire of an evening. It was hinted that she had been carried off by the Each Uisge, or Water Horse —a supernatural animal that frequented, and perhaps still frequents, the deep Hebridean lochs. In shape the Each Uisge resembled a dark and splendid horse, which in friendly fashion approached the lonely wayfarer and, having enticed the mortal upon his back, galloped with his victim to his loch, plunged beneath the peaty waters, and was no more seen. Or, it was suggested, the fairies—the Daoine Sith—had found the woman, and had put a spell upon her in one of their beautiful underground dwellings from which, of a moonlight night, comes the sound of music and dancing.

Summer merged imperceptibly into autumn.

Gradually the flowers upon the machair faded.
The crops ripened and were ingathered, and
then, one October day, a great company of
geese, on migration from their summer haunts
in far northern lands, were seen upon the
machair where the woman had disappeared.   At
evening they mounted into the soft air, continuing their journey south to the western Irish
coast, and, as before, the machair was lonely and
deserted.

For several years the mysterious Teine Mor
flitted hither and thither across the boggy heaths.
So greatly did it affect the nerves of the people
that only those having pressing business ventured
abroad after dark.

Then, as suddenly as it had appeared, the
light vanished, and now is seen no longer.

It may be that the woman has expiated her
crime of gathering a forbidden plant on the
Sabbath day, and has wandered with the sunset
to that land set beneath the horizon of the
Atlantic.   Here, in Tir nan Og, or the Land
of the Young, dwell Ossian, Diarmid, and
others of the Feinne—that band of chivalrous
warriors who had their era some fifteen hundred
years ago, and whose names still live and are

honoured wherever the Gaelic tongue is spoken. In Tir nan Og one may meet, in perpetual youth and in all the glory of their strength and beauty, many of those who are counted great and worthy of memory. On the shores of that land the surge breaks white, yet storms do not gather there, and the sun shines daily from a serene sky.

But whether or no the Teine Mor has voyaged thus far, or perchance dwells in that other immortal country, the Realm beneath the Waves, above which the great Atlantic billows thunder and the flood-tide and the ebb-tide flow tirelessly throughout the ages, the mysterious light, which some call the will-o'-the-wisp, has indeed gone from the Isles.

THE GREY CROW

No one has a good word to say for the grey or hoodie crow. He is hated by the game preserver because of the great damage he does to the eggs and young of grouse, partridges, and pheasants. By the shepherd he is equally detested, for he plucks the eyes from newly born lambs and any sheep that has fallen on its back and is unable to rise. Since every man's hand is against him, the hoodie has developed a nature of extraordinary wariness, and he is a far more difficult bird to photograph at the nest than the lordly and aloof golden eagle.

The hoodie has long been famed for his deceit.

There is an old Gaelic legend in the Isles that once there was in Uist an oyster-catcher who decided she would go out and see the world.

So she left her three eggs on the shingle and flew away. But a hoodie-crow came along, and thought the eggs would be a fine treat for him. He drove his bill through one of the eggs and carried it off, and was so pleased with it that he returned for the second egg, and then the third. The hoodie was taking his last suck of the last egg when the oyster-catcher returned. She could not find her eggs anywhere, and flew about crying out, " Who drank the eggs? Who drank the eggs? I never heard the like!" The grey crow gave an extra precautionary wipe of her bill, and flew up calling out with feigned sympathy, " Neither did I, although I have been long in the place!"

The hoodie does not lack impudence. A keeper in the Hebrides told me that he once saw it take a young bird from a merlin. And on another occasion he saw a common gull pick up a young mallard, and almost at once a grey crow flew up and pulled out one of the gull's tail-feathers. The outraged gull cried aloud in pain and anger, and then, of course, the young duck dropped from its mouth, and the crafty old hoodie swooped down, picked up the duckling, and ate it.

Each autumn and winter great numbers of hoodies migrate across the North Sea from Norway and Sweden, and make their winter quarters along the eastern shores of Scotland and England. But in the early spring these birds return overseas, and if one wishes to find the grey crow nesting in Britain in any numbers, one must go to the western seaboard of Scotland or to the Isles. Here there is little game preserving, and so the hoodie is less persecuted than elsewhere.

In the Outer Hebrides the grey crow cannot nest in trees, for the excellent reason that there are no trees for it to build on, and the nest is usually placed in the long heather of one of the innumerable islets on the many lochs of sea and fresh water.

One sunny day at the close of April a hoodie-crow and a grey lag-goose were found nesting together on a small island. There were six eggs in the grey lag's nest; the hoodie had just commenced to lay, and there was only one egg in her nest. Next day, on returning to the island, I found that the hoodie had laid her second egg, and had found and plundered the goose's nest. Five of the eggs she (presumably with her mate to help her) had sucked; the sixth they had been unable to finish, and it lay, half sucked, a few feet from the nest. Five weeks went past, then, one sunny June morning, I stripped and (the boat meanwhile being used on another loch) swam across to the hoodie's island, and found one young hoodie almost fledged in the nest. I gathered some long heather—cold work with a fresh and cool wind blowing and with the gatherer "in a state of nature"—and placed it near the nest, in order that the birds should become used to a hiding-tent a little later on. Four days later the hiding-tent was put up and covered with heather. The midges were abroad in such force in the windless air that every moment spent upon that island was a torture; but at length the tent was covered over with its "thatch" and a hurried departure was made, a bottle having been placed in a small hole in the front of the "hide" in order to accustom the hoodie to the camera lens later on. The work of the hoodies was visible in the neighbourhood. A red-throated diver's nest near contained one sucked egg, and not far away was a second nest, from which the eggs had also been removed. Five days after putting up the "hide" in position my wife and I commenced our attempts to photograph one of the most wary of all British birds. We assisted in dragging the boat to the loch, and, accompanied by the keeper, rowed across from the mainland and landed on the island. Both parent hoodies were very wild. Once or twice they flew over, high above us, then settled on a distant post of outlook, where they were almost invisible. I entered the "hide" and was covered in carefully by my wife, who rowed away ostentatiously, so as to distract the attention of the parent birds, at 10.30 a.m. When all was quiet, the young hoodie, which had been lying at the bottom of the nest, yawned, raised and stretched itself, then settled comfortably to doze. Nothing of interest happened during the first hour and a half, but at 11.50 the youngster "craaed" excitedly. The parent had evidently flown over, unperceived by me through the minute peep-hole in the "hide."

The youngster spent much time preening its feathers; once, when a great black-backed gull flew over, it imagined its mother was coming to feed it, and immediately was full of excitement. But the old hoodie was very suspicious, and it

was not until 12.55—that is, almost two and
a half hours after I had been shut into the
hiding-tent—that she suddenly appeared, standing in the short heather on the ridge about
a hundred yards from the nest. For fifteen
minutes she stood there doubtfully, then, when
I looked again, she was gone. She evidently
walked only a few yards away, for almost at
once she reappeared, walking along the ridge.
Three minutes later both parents appeared on
the ridge, and the fledgling " craaed " expect-
antly, hoping that its long-deferred meal was
at hand. But to its extreme chagrin they both
flew off. At last, just three hours after I had
entered the " hide," the mother hoodie again
appeared on the ridge, and almost at once flew
straight on to the nest and fed the young. I
was not more than twelve feet from her, so had
an excellent view of the feeding. The youngster
opened its mouth wide, and the mother thrust
her head far down its throat and fed it by
regurgitation. Immediately she had fed her off-
spring the hoodie flew off. Three-quarters of an
hour later she returned and again fed the young,
and after the feeding remained some seconds on
the nest and inspected the lens doubtfully.

My " watch " ended, and at 2.40 I was rowed
across to the mainland. At four o'clock I
returned. This time my wife was alone with
me in the boat, and after having covered me up
in the " hide," rowed across to the opposite
shore by herself. I commenced my second
watch—as it turned out, a very disappointing
one. The young hoodie played like a child,
picking up pieces of heather in its bill and
throwing them about. After I had been sitting,
doubled up, in my cramped quarters for an hour
and a half, both hoodies appeared on the ridge,
and with much " craaing " one (presumably the
cock) fed the other. But although the young
one shrieked loudly for food, standing up in the
nest and flapping its wings, the parents never
once came to the nest from 4.15 until I emerged
from the " hide," disgusted, at 7.40. It was
evident that they were able to count up to two
(this we proved to our satisfaction on the following day), and I am convinced they knew all the
time I was in the " hide," for they evinced great
anxiety whenever they flew near it, and when at
last I showed myself they became triumphantly
excited. It was as if they were shouting out
at me, " Ha, ha, we always knew you were in

there, but we are glad you have come out into the open where we can see you." In the nest was a grouse chick—very "high." This was the only food we ever saw at the nest, for, as I have said, the young was fed by regurgitation.

While I was awaiting the "relief" boat I walked round the island and found a number of sucked eggs beside the gull colony at the end of the island—evidently the work of the hoodies. The following evening, to test our theory that the hoodie can count (and, with the possible exception of the raven, it is the only British bird that can do so), I played a mean trick on the pair. It was my wife's "watch" in the "hide," and after rowing her across and concealing her in the hiding-tent, I rigged up two "dummies" made with our walking-sticks and oilskins, and set them up in the stern of the boat. Fearsome-looking objects they looked, and I am quite sure those hoodies were unusually thankful when I rowed the boat out of sight up the loch. So successful was my subterfuge that the crows flew backwards and forwards to the nest without suspicion that evening.

A HEBRIDEAN CAMP

June in the Outer Isles is a month without darkness. For perhaps two hours around midnight a soft twilight lies over the land and the winding lochs, but not until the beginning of August does true darkness come.

The Outer Hebrides is a country of innumerable lochs. There are sea-lochs and freshwater lochs, the latter so numerous that they form a maze out of which it is hard to find one's way.

Beside one of these lochs my wife and I pitched our tent early in June, amongst young green heather and the tender fronds of the bracken.

We were close beside the main road of the island, yet there was no house to be seen, and the eye rested on a great expanse of moorland with many lochs, and a range of hills bounding the horizon both east and west.

The bird-life of the Outer Isles is distinctive. Here one sees birds little known on the mainland, and as we sometimes lay awake in our tent at midnight we heard the curious far-carrying cries of red-throated divers flying across to the sea to their early morning fishing, or through the open flap of our tent could see other divers winging their way eastward in the rosy flush of the dawn to their small freshwater nesting lochans.

Alas, not for many nights did that tent-flap remain open !

We pitched our camp when the weather was cold and unusually wet. But the day after our arrival summer came suddenly to the Isles, and during our two weeks' camp we had uninterrupted warmth and sunlight. How delightful at first was the unaccustomed warmth ! Yet it brought with it a terrible pest—the Highland midge. At first these small insects appeared singly, then in twos and threes, and finally, as the heat became almost tropical, they increased to incredible swarms that rendered life a burden to us. At night they danced in dense clouds around our tent. Through the closed flaps, through tiny openings, they forced their way. Inside the tent they eagerly sought out their long-suffering prey, so that we were able to snatch brief intervals of sleep only by covering our heads with a towel and warily fashioning a small tunnel for a meagre supply of fresh air. Sunrises passed us unheeded; sunset of each day found us tightly enclosed in our tent, to which clouds of bloodthirsty insects eagerly and persistently sought admittance. In addition to the midges the heather swarmed with small ticks, which burrowed into our persons and added to our bodily discomfort.

One morning, when the sea mist lay close upon the hills and gave promise of a day of great heat, we were driven from the tent at five o'clock by the insupportable attacks of myriads of midges. These attacks were so fierce that it was impossible to dress within the tent; outside we found an eager, compact host awaiting us, and a few moments later any onlooker might have seen two apparently demented figures running backwards and forwards over the moor the while they hastily clothed themselves!

It was impossible to prepare breakfast; in desperation we rowed far out into the loch, and with our boat lying idly on the windless waters we fried our kippers, so thickly coated with midge corpses that they were scarcely recognisable. Our one cause for thankfulness was that the Outer Hebridean midge was decidedly smaller and less poisonous than his relative of Skye and the mainland.

Each day of our camping we used to pray for a breeze ; with joy we beheld far up the loch the slight ruffling of the glassy waters, which showed the approach of a current of air that would cause the midge world to take refuge in the grass and heather.

The loch beside which we camped penetrated, by way of narrow, shallow channels, for miles westward into the moorland.

On the loch were many islands, some covered with very old heather, in which grey lag-geese nested, others grassy, and the home of many sea-gulls.

As one approached these grassy isles in a boat, the gulls rose on white wings in a clamorous, drifting cloud. Above the high-pitched calling of the lesser black-backs one heard the deep, far-carrying bark of the sinister great black-backed gulls. A pair, or perhaps two, of these great gulls usually nested beside the colony—but on a small isle by themselves, where they ruled their little kingdom with none to dispute their sovereignty.

As one landed at the gull colony one heard the shrill pipe of oyster-catchers above the cries of the gulls. The oyster-catcher, an active and cheery bird, is plumaged in black and white, with long and ruddy bill that is used for probing in the sand and grass for worms, marine and terrestrial. "Saint Bride's servant," as the oyster-catcher is sometimes known in the Isles, is a tireless bird, and is just as full of life and music at midnight as at midday.

Besides the oyster-catchers, other "waders" nested with the gulls on these grassy isles. Sandpipers, sober-coloured birds with curious vibrating flight, protested at one's presence in a whistle even shriller pitched than that of the oyster-catcher, and dunlin—quaint black-breasted birds in size rather less than a snipe—made curious squeaky music, and stood near as one passed, as tame as barndoor fowls.

One evening when we were rowing homeward up the loch a short-eared owl rose from the farther side of an island on which very long heather grew, and with slow but powerful wing-thrusts pursued some trespassing gulls. The short-eared owl is the least nocturnal of Scottish owls ; he often hunts in daylight, especially if the day be a dull one, but when we saw him chasing the gulls, the sun was still shining brightly from a cloudless sky. From the behaviour of this old owl we made sure that his mate must be brooding her eggs or young somewhere on the island, and that evening we searched the isle without success, but found many pellets of the fur of mice and voles which the owls had cast up about the island. The following day we made further search, and put up old mother owl from our feet, where, in a narrow " runnel " between two rough and ancient heather-clumps, she had been brooding on her family of four owlets.

It is a curious characteristic of the owls that they lay their eggs at long intervals, and in this nest we found two newly hatched young owls and two elder members of the family at least ten days old. In the primitive nest were two short-tailed field voles, one rat, and one meadow pipit —all tucked away neatly in a little hollow at the side of the nest and in various stages of " high-ness." The sun shone brightly, and the young owls buried their heads in the nest to shelter themselves from the glare, the newly hatched chicks endeavouring to tuck their heads in beneath the thick down of the elder members of the family. If the babies became too restless, their big brothers and sisters pecked them to keep them in order.

During the time we were at the nest the cock owl circled overhead, making curious cries that sounded like elfin shouts or laughter rather than the call-notes of a bird. Sometimes he soared on the breeze, after the fashion of a buzzard. When the mother owl came to her babies she alighted on the ground some little distance from the nest, and crept up through the " runnels " between the old heather tufts so that her approach could not be observed. In like manner she noiselessly retreated when she heard the sound of approaching oars.

At the far end of the island was a merlins' nest. It, too, was in very long heather, and the merlins had chosen for their home an old nest of a grey crow, and had been content merely to add a few branches of heather to the derelict nest. There were two round eggs in the nest, and they were thickly covered with red markings.

Beside the nest we put up a hiding-tent, and watched and photographed the birds. Growing from the edge of the loch (the water was only a few yards distant, but rather below the nest) was a rowan tree—a tree that was formerly believed in the west to be a protection against certain occult powers. It was now laden with blossom, and the scent, drawn out by the heat and sunshine, hung with delightful fragrance on the dry air, so that even in the stuffy twilight of the " hide " one sensed its perfume.

One morning of sunshine I took up my station in the hiding-tent about ten feet from the nest. The " hide " was carefully covered over with heather, but the merlin was suspicious, and it was not until two hours and a half had gone by that he returned to the vicinity of the nest. He —for it was the cock merlin—alighted on the top of the long heather beside the nest, swaying in the breeze and doubtfully eyeing the lens of the camera which projected through the front of the "hide." What a charming picture he made —very light in plumage, dapper, and handsome. At length, his suspicions slightly lessened, he jumped down on to the eggs and shuffled them under him.

The nest was so deep that it hid him, all except his head : as he brooded his wife's eggs he reminded me of a diminutive fiery colonel, piercing of eye, nervy, and very gallant.

Later in the day, when the hen merlin took her turn on the eggs, I noticed that besides being larger than her mate (the hen of all raptores is larger than the cock) she was darker in the plumage. Both birds had beautiful large dark eyes—true falcon eyes.

On the farther shore of the loch the moorland stretched away as far as the eye could see. It was a boggy and, in misty weather, a dreary country, reminding me of the " tundra " of Spitsbergen ; so it seemed fitting to see that bird of Spitsbergen, the Arctic skua, speeding with strong flight above the sodden moor.

One evening, when rowing up the loch, we saw a skua sweep out over the water. It was chasing off a gull, and its behaviour showed that its nest must be near. We landed and walked over boggy moorland, on which a beautiful crimson orchis was blossoming, to where the skua had risen from the ground when, from a distance, it had seen us approach.

The slight nest on a small dry knoll contained

two dark heavily blotched eggs, and during the time that we were beside the nest both birds remained near, fluttering their wings helplessly as though to distract our attention from their eggs. The hen skua had the cheeks and breast white, or, more correctly, very light yellow ; the cock was sooty brown all over.

The Arctic skua is a delightful bird to photograph from a hiding-tent, for it is confident and fearless, and even the noise of a fast camera shutter fails to scare it from its eggs.

The following day I spent some hours in the " hide." The heat of the sun was so great that the water of the pools in the bog was actually hot to the bare feet. There was scarcely a breath of wind, and in the cramped quarters of the hiding-tent the heat was stifling. A very few minutes after my wife, having covered me carefully within the " hide," had returned to the loch, the hen skua alighted fearlessly beside her eggs and settled herself upon them, entirely ignoring the hiding-tent and the staring " eye " of the lens. So unsuspicious was she that she sometimes slept, with head thrown backward so that it rested upon the feathers of the back—a most unusual position for any bird to assume.

The skua is a bird pirate, and has in its eye
a true piratical expression.   It lives largely upon
fish, which it forces sea-gulls, terns, puffins, and
other victims to drop, pursuing these birds relent-
lessly this way and that until, in desperation,
they drop their hard-earned " catch," which the
skua dexterously retrieves in mid-air.

One morning, when the sun rose warm and
serene in the east and shed a soft light upon the
sentinel hills and wide moorlands, I crossed over
a heathery knoll where hooded crows were
clamouring and saw, east and west, a grey belt
of fog hang above the invisible sea.   Large,
brilliantly coloured dragon-flies darted like the
magic lances of Midir above the heather : the
milkwort, the sundew, the tormentil, the butter-
wort, and the red lousewort were all opening
their small, delightful flowers.   From a great
distance came the deep sound of the fog signal
on Neist Point on the Isle of Skye, showing that
across the Minch the fog lay closely.   But above
me the sky was cloudless, and from the little hill
I could see many lochs and lochans all lying
with glassy surface in the flood of soft, warm
sunlight.

A few hundred yards from me was a small tarn

holding a wee island a few feet from the shore. Here a red-throated diver was sitting on her eggs, and did not leave them although I passed close to her. The red-throated diver is a bird of the lesser Hebridean lochs; the larger lochs are frequented by the black-throated diver. And, perhaps because of the size of the lochs the two species haunt during the summer months, the habits of the two divers are different. The black-throated diver feeds usually on its own loch; the red throat goes to the sea for its fishing. Both divers are summer visitors to the Hebrides: they leave the lochs for the sea as soon as their young can fly.

It is now that the parent divers lose the handsome plumage of the nesting season, and when at sea are scarcely recognisable as the same birds that reared their young on some grassy island of a remote Hebridean loch.

During winter the divers range far south. On a February day I found one cast up by the tide on the beach at Sandwich. The crude oil afloat that has now become such a menace to all bird-life at sea had cost this black-throated diver its life. Its breast was matted with a coating of dried oil, so thick that it formed a rigid layer above the feathers, and it was surprising that the bird had been able to live so long in that condition.

In Scotland the red-throated diver is more wary than the black throat, but in Spitsbergen in the northern Arctic it is sometimes extraordinarily tame. There I photographed a red-throated diver without any concealment. Another sitting diver was even bolder, and used to snap viciously at anyone venturing close to her as she brooded her eggs. In that far northern land man is an intruder birds have not yet begun to fear. But even in the most remote of the Scottish Isles the divers have learned their lesson and are shy and suspicious.

Sometimes, on a misty night when from the leaden Atlantic the west wind drifted mysteriously across the boggy moorland, and when all was silent and very beautiful, the divers would fly, invisible in the mists, above our little camp to and from their fishing, and their hoarse cries, repeated excitedly in ever-faster succession, sounded extraordinarily loud and weird.

One stormy evening, when white-crested waves were racing across our loch, and when the midges had perforce to hide their unwelcome persons in the depths of the heather, a beautiful male hen-harrier crossed the waters near our tent. His pearly grey plumage caught the light of the setting sun ; with silent, easy flight he beat up against the wind, exploring each little hollow of the moor for any lurking rats or mice, and soon a ridge hid him from our view.

At sunset, when the air was almost still, we could sense the smell of the kelp fires on the western shores of the Isles. In fine weather the air was hazy with the pungent smoke of many such fires ; for the Isles folk were busy burning the winter-gathered seaware for the ash containing iodine and potash which the seaweed gives.

Sometimes at dusk the smell of aromatic peat fires from invisible dwellings was in the breeze, and we thought of the old Gaelic " rune " that in olden days was recited each night in so many humble sheilings of the Isles at the " smooring " of the peat fire.

At this simple and sacred rite the first peat was laid on the dimly burning fire in the name of the Spirit of Life, the second in the name of the Spirit of Peace, and the third and last in the name of the Spirit of Grace.

And meantime was recited in Gaelic the following lines :

> " The Sacred Three,
>   To Save,
>   To Shield,
>   To Surround,
>   The Hearth,
>   The House,
>   The Household,
>   This Eve,
>   This Night,
>   And Every Night,
>   Each Single Night.   Amen." [1]

[1] From *Carmina Gadelica*, by the late Alexander Carmichael, LL.D.

SEA MUSIC

"Mar chirein nan stuagh uaine ta mo ghaol."

"As the crests of the green waves is my beloved."

Old Gaelic Love Song.

As I write the south wind has been blowing strongly and steadily for four days. It has rushed across the Hebridean island of North Uist, lifting the water in spindrift from the peaty lochs and rocking the corn-stacks in its path. But—an unusual thing for the Outer Hebrides—the gale has brought with it no rain, no clouds, and the sun has shone continuously from a sky hazy with the salt spray of the disturbed Atlantic.

From the distant North Irish coast the south wind, with irresistible strength, wanders eagerly to the Western Isles of Scotland. On its path are the great cliffs of Barra Head and Mingulay. Across them the gale sweeps, then hurries onward to Barra Island and Eriskay (where in 1745 Prince Charles Edward first landed on British soil), and finds Hecla and Beinn Mhor of South Uist fair in its track.   How the tempest screams over the narrow ridge of Beinn Mhor, two thousand feet above the heaving Atlantic! Even a grown man is not safe here; he may be snatched from his scanty foothold and tossed far over the precipice that forms the northern face of Beinn Mhor.

Past the lochs of Houghmore sweeps the wind, and now it is lashing the waters that surround Benbecula.   From that isle the storm quickly arrives at North Uist, and as I pen these lines is making mournful music around the lodge.   From here I look out upon Houghary a mile seaward, and watch the great waves roll in one after the other, while the wind whips their crests from them and carries the spray far to leeward.

Northward of Houghary is a lonely bay where firm white sands rise from the edge of the tide to the bent grasses that grow thickly here. Even in fine summer weather the long ocean swell breaks on this wild shore in gleaming spray.   But as I write, in a time of winter storm, all the waters of the bay are churned into foam by the enormous waves which roll in on the flood-tide in a magnificent, unending army.

The waves are reaching their journey's end.

With majestic, unhurried rhythm the green quivering walls advance shoreward hour after hour. They near the sands and feel the shoal water. Like living things they rise quickly, and grow to a height of fully fifteen feet before they curl over and break with the deep roar of thunder.

How sublime is this Ceol Mara, this sea music! It seems to come to us from the approaches to Tir nan Og, on which the sun casts a flood of amber light when he dips behind the cliffs of distant Hirt, on the rim of ocean.

How wonderfully beautiful is the actual breaking of each wave! Slowly the high wall of green water curls over, hangs for an instant in space, then crashes down, imprisoning as it does so a layer of air between its crest and base. And as each wave breaks in spray, a transient rainbow is lighted above its crest, and (since the whole of the long wave does not break at the same moment) this spray-bow seems to dart magically from one end of the roller to the other.   As suddenly as they appeared the colours vanish and the wave is no longer afire.

Whence come these immense waves ?   How far into the Atlantic is their birthplace ?

Far west of Rockall—that lonely mountain-peak that just tops the waters one hundred and eighty miles west of Saint Kilda—the long Atlantic swell has its birth.   The waves that break on the white shores of Uist may the previous day have spouted high against Rockall, striking impotently against its dark rocks.

Of Rockall a curious story was told me recently by an officer of His Majesty's navy. During the Great War his ship was employed on convoy duty, and one dark night was steaming eastward towards her Scottish base, having escorted a west-bound convoy out beyond the submarine zone.   Suddenly ahead of her loomed up a dim, dark shape, apparently a vessel without lights.   The strange vessel seemed to be approaching, tossing the spray from her bows.   From my friend's ship the recognition signal was shown, and since it was ignored, " action quarters " was sounded and all was excitement, when suddenly it was seen that the supposed enemy vessel was Rockall !   At once the helm was put hard over, only just in time to avoid shipwreck.

On their lonely course to the eastern shores of Uist the waves have passed Saint Kilda with its sheer twelve-hundred-feet cliffs, and later on have rushed eagerly through Haskeir's mighty arches, where *ron mor*, the Atlantic seal, has his home.

How curious is the periodic lull that comes after a succession of great waves! The sea has almost freed itself from frothy foam, the thunder and rush of the surf are momentarily stilled, when a high wall of green water is seen approaching the shore. With unhurried speed it moves forward, momentarily becoming steeper and more menacing, until, breaking with terrible might, it rushes impetuously upon the strand.

As I listened to the sublime deep-toned music of the sea, a small company of bird-visitors passed unexpectedly across the stormy Atlantic. Flying, as is their custom, in the teeth of the gale, five barnacle geese steered south. At times they sped like shearwaters close above the water's surface, their background some great wave, green and white crested, against which their handsome black and white plumage was seen to perfection. Although two green cormorants,

8

steering the same course, had been brought momentarily to a standstill by the force of the wind, the geese forced their way southward against the gale at an astonishing rate. I am doubtful whether the eagle himself could have travelled so fast as they.

Whence had come the geese on this testing flight? From Shillay or Harris, perhaps, or from spray-drenched Gaisgeir, or mayhap even from far northern lands already in the grip of snow and frost.

Abroad upon the wild and foam-flecked waters were other birds. On back-bent wings a solan skimmed southward in the shelter of seas that towered but did not break ; in a turmoil of waters a cormorant fished, heedless of the surf that momentarily threatened to engulf it. Along the shore, wherever the rocks gave them shelter from the gale, bright-plumaged redwings fed, and from his bed among the bents a snipe sprang high into the air, and was instantly blown like a leaf at the mercy of the storm.

In the path of the oncoming seas one great rock stood sturdily. Through a narrow opening in it each wave rushed with a loud, hissing sound. Quickly the wave passed, and the rock, streaming white with frothy rivulets, emerged from the foamy maelstrom.

It is not only during southerly and south-westerly gales that the Atlantic waves sweep magnificently in upon the shores of the Isles. West winds bring mountainous breakers, and on some of the northerly Isles the north-west seas are heaviest of all.

It is curious that on the veering of the wind from west to north-west the ocean haze should vanish, and a steel-green heaven, set with vast *cumulus* or *nimbus* clouds of pale grey, stretch away and away to the heaving horizon. On the breath of these north-west storms thunder travels—for in the Isles thunder is a thing of winter rather than of summer, and comes almost always on a gale of west or north-west wind. With uncanny speed the storms of thunder and lightning sweep in towards the low spray-drenched shores. They strike the land, and a squall of hail sweeps the sodden fields with such violence that neither man nor beast can stand against it. The lightning is vivid, but the roll of the thunder can scarce be heard above the roar of the wind and the hiss of the hail-stones. But quickly the storm passes away to leeward, and the winter sun once more sheds his pale beams over the land.

And what of *Gaoth Tuadh*, the north wind, and his three sons that were named White Wings, White Feet, and White Hands?

White Feet wanders swiftly down upon the Isles from the blue ice-masses which lie always upon the breast of the Greenland ocean. It is the tread of White Feet upon Hebrid seas that churns the Atlantic into short-crested seas so that the westerly swell is broken up and rushes in no more upon Haskeir nan Ron.

In the Isles the north wind is a fine-weather wind, and brings with it sharp invigorating air, so that even the most distant rocks and isles stand out clearly.

In the blue sky white clouds sail southwards. The ocean, and each peaty loch, reflect the blue of heaven. The surf upon outpost reefs gleams white, and even in autumn larks mount into the country of the air with joyous song.

By the people of the Isles the north wind, provided it be not too boisterous, is greeted with pleasure. By none is it more appreciated than the crew of the small mail-boat, for in the Minch the northerly seas are seldom heavy.

But of late years the north wind in winter has rarely held for more than a day or two at a time. Towards evening on the second, if not indeed of the first, day of its life, the black wind (as the north wind is sometimes called) drops to the lightest of airs. The Isles are bathed in a soft rosy glow; the peat smoke rises in thin blue columns into the serene sky, where, one by one, the planets and the fixed stars light their lamps. At nightfall a band of pale light burns on the northern horizon and sends out ghostly streamers towards the zenith. These are the Northern Lights or the Merry Dancers, and there is a legend in the west that when the fallen angels were cast out of heaven, one company became the Fairies, a second the Blue Men that of a moonlight night play shinty on the waters of the Minch, and the third the Northern Lights.

The Merry Dancers almost always herald a change of weather, and before dawn the crisp air and the clear skies are gone, and our old friend the south wind is sweeping with momentarily increasing speed across the misty shores of the Isles.

A HEBRIDEAN SEA-POOL

On the west side of the island of North Uist is a small inlet of the Atlantic. Its name is Loch Paible, and not so many years ago it was a freshwater loch. But an attempt to drain the loch allowed the Atlantic to force an entrance, and now at high tide it is a sea loch, but at the ebb is a muddy basin, with a very small trickle of water running through it. At its seaward end the loch narrows, and at half-ebb and half-flood a heavy volume of water pours through the channel here. But as the tide recedes the flow of water quickly lessens, until, an hour or so before low water, a deep pool becomes visible with a moderate stream of water flowing through it.

This is the sea-pool of which I write.

There are scores of sea-pools in the Hebrides which yield larger sea-trout, yet none can surely excel this small sea-pool of Loch Paible in the attractiveness of its surroundings, with the smell of its seaweed mingling, of a late summer day, with the scent of the ragwort and the innumerable lesser flowers of the surrounding machair.

It was late one August evening when first I saw the sea-pool of Loch Paible. The tide was far out, and the pool lay altogether still in the windless air of an island sunset. Scarcely a trickle of water entered the pool, and in the clear depths, unruffled by a breeze, fishing was useless.

Out to sea lay the Monach Islands of the golden sands. A few hundred yards from the sea-pool tiny waves broke lazily upon the beach, and here a couple of men were wading almost thigh-deep. They carried pitchforks, and were attempting to spear flounders. Without success they walked slowly backwards and forwards until, tiring of their chilly and profitless occupation, they left the water and made their way to the sea-pool. Their surprise appeared considerable when they learned that I was after sea-trout, and not flounders. They suggested that I should bait my fly with lug-worms, for then, they said, I might entice some large flounder from the depths of the pool where it had been lying half buried in the fine sand.

There was one particular spot, they said, where a flounder was almost always to be found, and to convince me, one of the men waded deep into the pool and, taking careful aim, quickly plunged his pitchfork beneath the water. But he must have misjudged the spot, for the prongs of his implement impaled no flounder, but struck an invisible rock with rasping sound. Somewhat discomfited, the man and his companion walked homeward across the machair, and once more I had the sea-pool to myself.

Dusk imperceptibly deepened and many flights of birds passed overhead. The evening silence was broken by the high-pitched whistle of whimbrel, the wild fluting call of a passing greenshank, the wail of green plover, and the weird, uncanny cries of many curlew. From time to time the placid surface of the pool was broken by a leaping sea-trout that showed as a silver bar in the fading light. Imperceptibly the tide turned, and crept stealthily up the shore, entering the pool at first hesitatingly, then in greater volume, as darkness settled over the isle.

From an azure sky in which a few clouds

floated the sun shone early next morning as I
made my way across the machair to the sea-pool.
Northward lay Haskeir, with its small rocky isles
to the south of it.   These lesser rocky isles are
the home of innumerable sea-fowl ; seen from a
distance they resemble a row of peat-stacks set
by some giant hand in Atlantic depths.   Southward the hills of South Uist formed the horizon ; west Saint Kilda showed faintly above the
Atlantic plain.

Across the machair a female hen-harrier flew
with leisurely gliding flight.   As she crossed a
reed-covered bog I saw her flight become more
rapid.   She now urged herself forward with
powerful, clean-cut wing-thrusts, and just ahead
of her I saw a red-necked phalarope endeavouring to escape from the hawk.   The phalarope
—a bird rather less than a snipe in size—flew
so swiftly that the harrier soon abandoned the
pursuit, and perched upon a rock, where she
commenced leisurely to preen her feathers.

For the angler each sea-pool has its own little
peculiarities, but there is one rule that is almost
constant, namely, that the sea-trout cease to
" take " once the salt waters of the flood-tide
have reached, and flowed through, the pool.

Above the sea-pool of Loch Paible a moderately shallow rapid (flowing, of course, inland) is formed at the earlier stages of the flood-tide. This broken water extends for perhaps eighty yards, and about half an hour after the tide has entered the pool the sea-trout leave it and swim to the stretch of quick-running water, leaping high into the air as they do so. Until the run of water becomes too heavy the sea-trout will sometimes take the fly here, but the angler must stand well back from the water and use fine tackle, for the water is so clear that the fish readily see the fisherman on the bank. As the tide continues to flow and the body of water increases in volume, the fish apparently now pass into the quickly filling Loch Paible, and fishing is then useless. At the flood of a spring tide the loch is a wide sheet of water, extending almost to Balranald Lodge.

When the tide turns the first of the ebb brings down a great body of water through the neck of the loch, and for fully three hours the sea-pool is invisible in a waste of rushing waters. And even when the sea-pool becomes a pool once more, the sea-trout do not settle down until the flow of water has decreased to an insignificant volume. By this time the pool has become clear, and a strong breeze is essential for successful fishing, in order that the water should be well agitated and the angler and his line invisible. There is, it is true, a short period between sunset and darkness when the pool may be fished, even in a dead calm, but it is not often that the tide suits exactly at this time.

In the dusk of a summer evening when no breeze stirred I once reached the sea-pool. The tide was just right, and a number of fine sea-trout were showing in the shallow water at the head of the pool, where they had collected in order to taste the fresh water that is mingled with the salt at low tide.

Had there been broad daylight at the time the fish would have been disturbed by the first cast and would have returned to the deep waters of the pool; but in the dusk they saw neither the line nor the angler, and each time the fly was drawn across them a fish would follow it and just touch it. I have found that under these conditions one frequently loses a sea-trout by striking too soon, and I believe the fish has more chance of being hooked if the fly be momentarily slowed down when the sea-trout is seen to be following it. But it must be remembered that if the fly is slowed down too much the fish instantly becomes suspicious, and swerves off. On the particular evening of which I write the fish were very wary, but at last, after a number of misses, I was into a good one. He fought well, and when at last he was landed turned the scales at two pounds. Like all the fish of the sea-pool he was perfectly clean run, with many sea-lice adhering to him. This fish in his wild dashes for liberty so disturbed the pool that no further sea-trout showed until darkness put an end to fishing.

The next morning, with a dark and stormy sky and half a gale blowing up from the south, the sea-pool was in good fishing order, and I landed another two-pounder, a very fine thick fish which played even better than the sea-trout of the evening before. On this day the air was so hazy that the hills of South Uist were scarcely visible, and in the early afternoon the wind increased in violence, bringing in an exceptionally high tide that remained longer than usual in the loch. An hour before sunset the rain suddenly ceased, the wind veered from south to west, and from the grey leaden skies the

clouds magically evaporated. The tide should
have suited the sea-pool that evening, but the
strong wind had held up the ebb to such an
extent, that as I crossed the machair to the loch
I saw that there would be little chance of fishing.
On the rain-sodden machair many larks' ran
ahead of me. They were unwilling to take
wing and kept to the track, which was comparatively dry. Flocks of golden plover—that are
known in the Gaelic as *feadagan*—sped this way
and that, and an unusually large assembly of sea-
gulls were resting beside the tide. As the daylight waned the full moon, low on the southern
horizon, shone with soft and ruddy light from a
velvety sky. In her mellow beams the waters
of the sea-loch showed as burnished gold. That
evening dusk fell imperceptibly, for sunset and
moonlight gradually merged with no lessening
of the light. On arriving at the sea-pool I saw
at a glance that no fishing would be possible
before the last of the daylight faded. Where
the pool should have been, a great river rushed
seaward, with glittering moonbeams playing
upon the turbulent waters. Many birds were
abroad. Across the moon a flock of bar-tailed
godwits passed, calling to one another with soft

musical notes. For an instant they were transformed to birds of gold, then passed into the impenetrable dusk. Immediately above me a curlew crossed, flying very low, and suddenly the night air was vibrant with his wild impetuous song. Out to sea, far beyond where the line of breakers showed white on outlying reefs, the darkness was stabbed by the rhythmic rays of the Monach light.

As summer merged into autumn most of the sea-trout left the sea-pool. Many, no doubt, cruised round the coast and entered Loch Horisary ; others passed up the moorland stream and arrived in the peaty waters of Loch Vausary. The weather, too, became wilder, and frequent gales, from west, north, and south, churned the surface of the sea-pool so that crested wavelets raced madly across it. There were days when the sailing boat from the Monach Isles made the passage with difficulty.

Laden with mail and provisions for that lonely island group, she left her anchorage close to the sea-pool and, pitching and rolling giddily, shot out from the shelter of the rock into a white-crested turbulent sea. Then even the sturdy solans had difficulty in moving against the wind, and flew grimly and with great effort a few feet above the angry, racing waves. But sometimes, for a few short hours, the wind dropped light, the sky was clear and blue, and the Atlantic reflected and seemed even to intensify the blue abysses of the zenith.

At times such as these a mirage was formed, and the neighbouring isles and even the houses of Benbecula seemed to be suspended miraculously in air. It was then that hills, isles, and ocean made a fairyland of beauty, and those fleeting and magic hours more than compensated for the wind and rain that so often crossed the isle of the sea-pool.

A HEADLAND OF THE ISLES

AT the extreme north-westerly edge of North Uist a lonely headland stands. Its name is Griminish Point, and even in summer it is a wild and very solitary place. In winter the Atlantic surf breaks constantly upon its dark rocks and thunders through the caves from which blue rock-pigeons dart.

November has brought wintry weather to the Outer Isles this season of which I write, and as I pen these lines the north wind carries winter on its breath, and squalls of snow and hail drive in from the ocean.

From Balranald to Griminish the way leads through cultivated land, and the crofters were busy leading their crop this bright November morning. Sadly battered by the storms, the sheaves of oats and barley lay in the fields. In some instances the husks as well as the grain had been torn off the oat plants, and the bare stems alone remained. A November harvest in the Isles is a rare event, and means much hardship for the people during the winter and spring months.

As I write, the peats still lie ungathered out on the sodden moors. The rough tracks to the peat mosses have been so softened by continuous rains that carts cannot be driven along them to bring home the fuel, and so the peats must be carried laboriously for miles in a creel or in a sack. As the peat moss is often several miles from the crofting township, it will be realised how arduous a task this is.

How changed is the machair by recent storms! In September it was bright with flowers. Gentian, ragwort, eyebright, scabious—to name only a few—threw a wave of colour over all the level grazing land. Now even the hardy ragwort has been killed, and the machair is brown as the tundra of the Arctic after the melting of the winter snows.

Coinneach Odhar, the Brahan seer, foretold many things concerning the Highlands. One of his prophecies was that the day would come when the Isles would be depopulated by

9

driving rain. Did he visualise the two great
emigrations of 1923 and 1924? Who amongst
those who witnessed them will ever forget
the sorrowful scenes upon the pier at Loch
Boisdale when the great liner *Marloch* transported to Canada upwards of two hundred
men and women from Barra, South Uist, and
Benbecula, and when, the following spring,
she carried westward over the Atlantic another
sorrowful company? Let us hope, for the
sake of the isles-folk, that the succession of
incredibly wet summers is at an end.

Immediately above Griminish Point is a
low heathery hill. Its name is Beinn Scolpaig,
and from its top is a wide and varied view.
As I climbed the gradual slope, spongy and
sodden with the rain of months, a squall of
snow drifted in from the Atlantic, hiding the
wintry sun and whitening the heather and the
brown hill grasses. Swiftly across the hill a
merlin sped; below me a flock of golden
plover circled. The constant rain has driven
the migrant snipe from their accustomed
haunts. One sees them in unlooked-for
places. Only last week I surprised a number
of these birds sheltering together on the sand

of the shore just above high-water mark, and to-day snipe were on the relatively dry ground on the top of Beinn Scolpaig. One bird behaved exactly as a young snipe might have done. It jumped up at my feet, and ran a few yards ahead of me as though unable to fly. I had decided that it was wounded, when it rose suddenly with swift erratic flight and disappeared over the hilltop.

From the summit of Beinn Scolpaig the scene was a wild and very wintry one. North-west heavy seas were breaking upon Haskeir. Directly behind Haskeir the cone of Saint Kilda showed faintly, but soon was veiled in a quick-travelling snow squall. North rose the Harris hills, their snowy slopes contrasting sharply with the dark skies beyond them. Nearer at hand was the Sound of Harris with its many islands. Upon Shillay, the most outlying of them all, the sun shone brightly, lighting up the spray from the great seas that broke rhythmically against its lonely shore.

As I descended to Griminish Point the short winter afternoon was drawing to a close. Against the wind the spring tide flowed in swiftly, raising a short and steep sea that broke in spray, time after time, against the grim headland. The spray rose, dazzling white, in the sunlight. For a second it showed all the brilliant colours of a rainbow, then was borne away on the breeze.

In late summer great numbers of solan geese pass in an unending procession close inshore at Griminish Point. At that season the waters of the Atlantic are warm, and many fish are showing near the coast. But by November the herring and mackerel are no longer near the surface, and the solan has almost deserted the coast of Uist. To-day I saw but one *sulaire* (to give the solan its Gaelic name), and it was flying quickly west, moving aslant the wind and skimming the waves with graceful motion. It glided along each white crest, and followed awhile each deep trough unerringly. From its purposeful flight I suspected it to have been on migration. A glaucous gull passed the headland, flying in the teeth of the strong breeze. The glaucous gull is not unlike the herring gull, but is larger, and lacks the black tips to the wings. It is a winter visitor—and never a common one—to us from the Arctic, and its

unexpected appearance off this Hebridean headland brought back memories of the isles and
cliffs of Spitsbergen—for it was there that I
last saw the glaucous gull at its Arctic nesting-
haunts.

On one of the ledges of rock of Griminish
Point was an old raven's nest, built entirely
of the stems of laminarian seaweed. The
birds themselves were absent and may have
travelled eastward, for in autumn the raven
sometimes visits the central Highlands in
large flocks. The birds are attracted thither
by the *greallach* of the deer, and remain in
that inland district only a short time.

On Griminish Point in autumn are seen the
deadly effects of the sea-spray on all land
vegetation. On the exposed headland the
plants of sea-thrift were browned and to all
appearances lifeless, yet in sheltered hollows,
out of reach of the spray, a green carpet
covered the ground, and in niches of the
rocky walls of the caves the scurvy grass
(Cochlearia) was almost as luxuriant as at
midsummer.

In a small hollow among the rocks a
redshank was dozing. Unexpectedly I came

upon him, and with wild whistlings he flew
off, his clear cries of alarm echoing and re-
echoing amongst the rocks.   Over the sea
a kittiwake battled with the wind, and a shag
made laboured headway just above the water.

Behind the Monach Isles the wintry sun
dipped, and against the sun-flushed sky the
lonely lighthouse showed as a sharp needle-
like object.   On the southern horizon rose the
three big hills of South Uist.   They were
snow-clad, and across one of them—Corodale—
the drifting powdery snow could be seen to
rise as a thin cloud high above the hilltop.
On a field beside the headland a flock of
twites were feeding, and one of them was an
almost pure white bird.

Dusk fell, but the work of ingathering the
harvest continued, for at last the precious crop
had been dried by the keen wintry wind, and
men and women were busy in the fields so
long as any daylight remained.   As I passed
the growing stackyards I heard the whistling
of lively pipe tunes, and saw the sheaves being
tossed by hand to the mounting stacks upon
which bearded men stood and adjusted the
stooks with the skill of many years.

At the coming of darkness the wind blew yet more chill, and in the northern sky the pale shafts of the aurora flickered, dimming the light of the stars that shone through the frosty air.

THE ATLANTIC SEAL

OFF the coast of Scotland and the Isles are
found two species of seals, the great grey or
Atlantic seal and the common seal.   Of the two
the Atlantic seal is very much the larger, and
there was once shot a bull seal of this species
which weighed no less than forty-nine stone.

The Atlantic seal is a lover of the open
sea ; the common seal frequents sea-lochs and
the more sheltered waters of the ocean.   In
their habits the two seals differ widely.   The
common seal gives birth to its pup in early
summer, and the infant seal is immediately
at home in the water.   The young grey seal,
on the other hand, is born in autumn.   It is
dropped by its mother above the reach of an

ordinary high tide, and, unless alarmed, it does not enter the sea until it is a month or six weeks old. And thus, during the first month of its life, an Atlantic seal pup is helpless and falls an easy prey to an enemy. Officially the Atlantic seal is protected during the time she is rearing her young, but many fishermen are unaware of the Grey Seals' Protection Act, and are none too anxious to make themselves acquainted with it. For centuries the crofter-fishermen of the Isles have sailed every autumn when the weather was favourable to one isolated rocky island where a colony of Atlantic seals have their nursery. But the last time—a few years ago—a boat was there it had a narrow escape from being swamped in the heavy sea that suddenly arose, and since then the seal people have been unmolested.

More than two hundred years ago the annual battue of Atlantic seals took place, for Martin writes in 1703 :

" On the Western Coast of this Island (North Uist) lyes the Rock Cousmil, about a quarter of a mile in circumference, and it is still famous for the yearly fishing of Seals there, in the end of October. This rock belongs to the

Farmers of the next adjacent Lands, there is
one who furnisheth a boat, to whom there is
a particular share due on that account besides
his proportion as Tenant ; the Parish Minister
hath his choice of all the young Seals and
that which he takes is called by the Natives
Cullen Mory, that is the Virgin Mary's Seal.
The Farmers man their boat with a competent
number for the business, and they always im-
barque with a contrary wind, for their security
against being driven away by the Ocean, and
likewise to prevent them from being discovered
by the Seals, who are apt to smell the scent of
them and presently run to sea.   When the Crew
is quietly landed, they surround the Passes,
and then the signal for the general attacque
is given from the Boat and so they beat them
down with big staves.   The Seals at this On-set
make towards the sea with all speed, and often
force their passage over the necks of the stoutest
assailants, who aim always at the Forehead of
the Seals, giving them many blows before they
be killed.   The Natives told me that several of
the biggest Seals lose their lives by endeavouring to save their Young ones, whom they
tumble before them, towards the Sea.   I was

WRAPPING UP THE FLEECE AFTER A DAY'S CLIPPING

IN THE OLD BLACKHOUSE COWS SHARED THE ENTRANCE

A SEAL PUP

SEAL COWS ANXIOUS FOR THEIR CALVES

A BULL ATLANTIC SEAL

SURF CREAMING INTO A HEBRIDEAN BAY

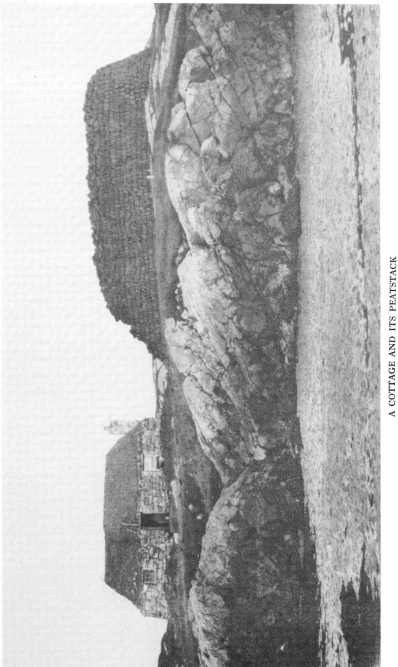

A COTTAGE AND ITS PEATSTACK

THE CORN OF THE MACHAIR LAND

HARVESTING BY HAND

A SHIELING

STACKING PEATS

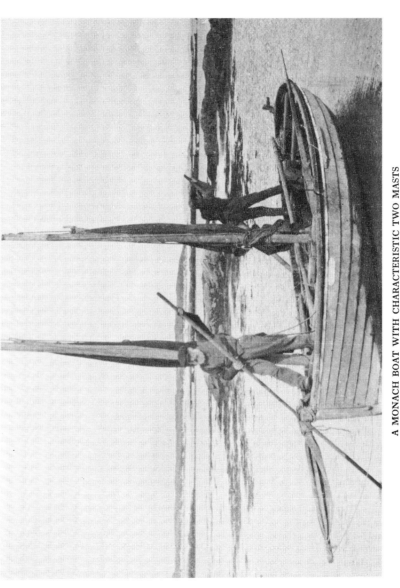

A MONACH BOAT WITH CHARACTERISTIC TWO MASTS

SHEARING SHEEP ON PABBAY, BY BARRA

LOBSTER FISHER'S CRAFT

GATHERING SEAWEED FOR USE AS MANURE

THRESHING OATS FOR SEED WITH THE OLD FLAIL

A PRIMITIVE ISLAND HOUSE

THE ATLANTIC SEAL   139

told also that 320 Seals, Young and Old, have been killed at one time in this Place."

Probably because of these attacks the Atlantic seal has abandoned the "Rock Cousmil," or Cousamul as it is to-day spelled, and now rears its young upon the less accessible isles. The Atlantic surf guards these isles well from human trespassers.

I shall always remember my first visit to a crowded nursery of the Atlantic seal. For three weeks I had waited on a neighbouring inhabited island for fine weather. One evening from a hill I looked across to the isle of the seals. The west wind blew strongly and fountains of spray rose from the isle, grey against the sullen horizon. My steamer for the mainland sailed the following afternoon, and my chances of seeing the seals seemed hopeless. But that evening about midnight the wind shifted north-east with heavy squalls of hail, and when at dawn next morning I looked out across the Atlantic the air was windless, the sky serene and clear, and the white-crested waves rolled slowly in, one after another, upon the low sandy shore. The swell was quickly subsiding, and the boatmen were willing to make an attempt to reach the island of the grey seals.

It was November. From a deep blue sky the sun shone with almost summer heat. Westward, on the rim of ocean where Saint Kilda showed, a layer of white cumulus clouds seemed to tower from the blue waters. North and east were high hills that gleamed white with unbroken snow. Into the blue sunlit sea we sailed. Our course at first was through a maze of islands. It was necessary for us to pass between two of these islands by way of a tide-swept sound. The tide was very low at the time, and the heavy swell sweeping into the sound from the north-west threatened to break in the shallow water. A crested wave would have been disastrous to our small craft, and when a great wave did curl over ahead of us right in our course, the boatmen spoke excitedly among themselves in Gaelic, and debated whether they should put about. Up the great flanks of the advancing waves we climbed giddily, but, fortunately for us, no second wave broke until we had sailed beyond the danger zone and were steering west through deep waters that showed a very dark blue. Ahead of us was now visible the island whither we were bound. It was lit up with the soft golden sun-

shine of the west, and the snowy spray that
from time to time sprang high into the still
air gleamed and glistened.

As we neared the island we lowered our
sail lest the seals should see it and take fright,
and very cautiously approached the shore.
Near the centre of the isle the rocks gave place
to a gently sloping sandy beach, and we could
see many Atlantic seals, both old and young,
basking on the sun-warmed sand. Behind this
pleasant shore, on the western side of the
narrow isle, the surf broke constantly, and in
the calm air the spray hung above the rocks.
It even mounted far up the hillside above them,
and was suspended there as morning mist lies
in some silent glen of a midsummer dawn.
Suddenly from the sea around us were thrust
the great heads of the seal-folk, and solemn,
questioning eyes watched us as we made ready
to land.

Upon a grassy slope above the beach a numerous
company of barnacle geese stood. They gazed
at us uncertainly, for no boat had touched at
the island since they had left their summer
haunts in Greenland or Spitsbergen, and it was
not until some time after we had landed that

they rose in a body and filled the air with musical calls as they complained to one another of our presence.

It was dead low water when we landed and a large area of sand was exposed. We went ashore some distance from the beach, and then stalked the seals which dozed on the sandy shore. On seeing us, those seals nearest to the water hurried with shuffling gait into the sea, but a number of the animals were too far from the water to make their escape, and these eyed us doubtfully as they kept their ground. There seemed to be no "look out" among the seals, and we came upon some of the colony lying on broken rocky ground which had hid our approach from them. These animals had no warning of our coming, and eyed us with sudden alarm. Side by side two seals were lying beside a rock. One of them was black, the other a silvery grey. The skin of the silvery-grey seal hung loosely in folds ; she seemed to be very old.

For a moment they lay there, full of anxiety. Then, with deep moaning roars they charged us, and it was impossible to keep them back from the sea.

Beyond the beach was a strip of boulder-strewn ground. Above the boulders was a comparatively level area covered with short grass, and beyond that, again, short heather and peat-hags. Over all this ground Atlantic seals were lying. Some were of enormous size; almost all of them were near their pups. But as we approached them, all the mother seals except one left their youngsters and made for the sea. This one seal guarded her young with supreme devotion. She allowed me to approach to a distance of about ten feet; nearer than that she would not permit me to come, and lunged towards me menacingly, opening her mouth wide and uttering hollow roars. From time to time her pup bleated like a lamb, and then she turned anxiously towards it, her thoughts momentarily distracted from her own plight. The young seal lay in the shelter of a log of driftwood, its white silky coat stained grey with peat.

On the grassy " flat " was a small peaty tarn. In this tarn two huge seals were swimming. One of the seals, no doubt excited by our appearance, set upon the other, and a desperate struggle began. The black waters of the tarn were churned into foam as the seals sprang one upon the other and gripped each other with their teeth. Quickly the battle ended, and side by side the two huge seals raced (if such a word may be used to describe their laboured but astonishingly rapid progress) from the tarn to the sea.

In a large pool beside the tarn a number of grey seal pups were hiding, and with them one old mother seal. The pups, although not more than a month or six weeks old, were able to remain below the surface for long intervals. Occasionally the long retriever-like head of the old seal showed on the surface for a second or two, then, after silently looking round, was drawn beneath the water. All over the island the old Atlantic seals were cautiously making their way to the sea from the nurseries. But the seal pups were too young to follow them. Singly, in couples, in threes and fours, they lay on the short grass that was trampled and flattened down by their weight. In the air was a bleating as though many lambs were calling, and in this plaintive calling and the clamour of the barnacle geese as they passed often overhead was a wild musical harmony very pleasant to hear.

Some of the grey seal pups lay on their backs
fast asleep in quaint attitudes.   They were
absurdly fat, and a number of them showed not
" double chins," but quadruple and quintuple
chins !

So soundly did they slumber that it was
possible to walk quietly up to them and photograph them without arousing them from their
siestas ! The pups were of different ages.   Some
of them were not more than a week old, and
were clad in the long white silky fur that is
worn only for the first week after birth.   Their
eyes were large and very dark brown.

Other pups had grown their second coat—thick
cream-coloured fur, rather short and curly ; while
the oldest of them had already assumed the third
coat—dappled grey, and not unlike the adult
seals' fur in colour.

But although some of the pups were at least
six weeks old, none of them showed any inclination to take to the sea, and it is said that the
only thing that causes them to enter the Atlantic
during the first two months of their lives is an
intense frost.

It is believed by scientists that the grey seal
was much more recently a land animal than the

common seal ; hence the terrestrial habits of the seal pups. Certainly when one remembers that the young common seal swims actively the first day of its life, the difference in their behaviour is striking.

As we crossed the nursery we noticed how varied was the colouring of the older seal pups. Some were almost black, though slightly dappled. Others were of a pale brownish yellow, and a few cream-coloured like the younger pups.

In a delightfully clear rock-pool a number of young seals were swimming (for though they do not take to the open sea during the early stages, they readily enter the shallow and tranquil water of a rock-pool). These pups were perhaps two months old, yet showed little alarm at our approach. As we watched them they frequently came to the surface and swam, with the whole head above the water, backwards and forwards across the pool, the sunshine causing their wet heads to glisten. Behind the pool dark rocks rose ; beyond these rocks lay the sun-kissed Atlantic plains. One after the other great waves hurled themselves ponderously upon the isle, shattering themselves in spray upon the grim barrier of rock which had for so many centuries withstood them. In the air was suspended a film of spray, dimming the middle view. No wilder or more magnificent scene can be pictured than the view that sunny November day from this island outpost where the Atlantic seals rear their young.

Across the short grass the mother seals had worn many paths as they had visited their pups to suckle them, and upon the grass lay the shed fur of the youngsters. I noticed that two of the pups had lost an eye—perhaps pecked out by grey crows—and that two baby seals lay dead at the edge of the grassy "flat."

Wherever one walked were young Atlantic seals. They must have numbered at least three hundred. Near the centre of the island a wee burn had its source, and flowed to the peaty tarn in a series of pools. In each peaty pool seal pups wallowed, and had pressed upward to the springs of the burn. Some of these youngsters at our approach submerged the head in the peaty slime. They evidently believed, like the ostrich, that if they could no longer see us we could no longer see them. Others submerged more carefully, but were betrayed by their backs rising from the water. In the pools they crowded and splashed as though they were giant salmon pressing up to their moorland spawning beds.

On the flood-tide we sailed away from the island of the seals. The breeze had freshened from the north-east and the sun was dipping westward, flooding the corries of the snowy hills to the north that stood out like mountains of the Arctic. In the sunset the many isles seemed to glow with the soft mystic light of the west, and over the waters was wafted the pleasant scent of peat fires as one by one the stars appeared and the Milky Way spread, like a shaft of the Merry Dancers, across the zenith.

Again after the lapse of a twelvemonth we sailed out to the grey seals' nursery. On the calm waters were swimming many black guillemots and long-tailed ducks, and as we neared the isle a great northern diver flew swiftly ahead of us. As before, the barnacle geese fed upon the grassy slopes of the island, and many grey seals dozed on the sandy beach. Upon a rock, fast asleep in the sun, lay an old bull seal. I stalked him with a camera, and succeeded in photographing him just before my nailed boots slipped on the rock and awoke the sleeper with a start.

He seemed mildly surprised but not alarmed, and without undue haste dragged his great bulk to the sea.

Perhaps a hundred and fifty yards from the tide was a pool of dirty fresh water. In this pool a number of seal pups were lying, and on a tiny island in the pool a purple sandpiper was asleep. We had approached to within eight feet of him before he awoke, and even when he saw us he did not take wing but, seeming scarcely to believe his eyes, fluttered to the shore and watched us with calm surprise. This small sandpiper must have travelled far, since his clan does not nest in Scotland, but in the Arctic. At the approach of autumn the purple sandpipers fly south, and winter on the isles and upon mainland shores.

As we neared the beach, the seals, just as they did a year before, scrambled to the water. Even on land they moved considerably faster than a man can walk, but once in the sea their speed increased, and they sped forward, the tail of each churning the shallows like the propeller of a lightly loaded steamer. Immediately they reached sufficiently deep water they dived swiftly.

After they had recovered from the excitement of that first mad rush for safety they swam cautiously inshore, and from time to time a crowd of dark heads eyed us. One old seal was unusually anxious about her pup. She cruised backwards and forwards along the edge of the tide, then (since we remained motionless) slowly dragged herself out of the sea and lay with the small waves washing over her. Again I saw a fierce fight. Perhaps because we disturbed her, one of the mother seals encroached upon the territory of another and thus the fight commenced. With deep moaning cries of rage the assailants struck at one another. Soon it was seen that one of the seals was severely bitten. Her thick neck was raw and streamed with blood, and during each breathing space in the fight she took the opportunity of rolling herself seaward very, very slowly. She did this in order, I think, that her antagonist should not realise her intentions of escaping. Suddenly the animals saw me standing a few yards from them and paused in their battle, and the wounded seal quickly reached the sea and submerged her gory neck, tingeing the waters with red.

On the western side of the island a seal pup

was lying fully sixty feet above the sea. The
rocks here dropped almost sheer to the Atlantic,
and each time the mother came up to suckle
her young she must have had a trying climb.
Looking over the cliff, we saw the mother seal
lying sound asleep on a rock near the water's
edge. I set out to "stalk" her, and, profiting
by my experience with the old bull seal, removed
my boots before starting. I reached the seal
without awakening her, and stood looking at her,
lying three feet from me. After a time violent
tremors ran through her body, as if in her
sleep she sensed something of my nearness. At
last she awoke, stared up at me an instant in
astonishment, then sprang in a swift dive to the
friendly water a dozen feet below.

No one who has watched the Atlantic seals
at close quarters can fail to be impressed by the
intelligent expressions of some of the animals,
and among the people of the isles these great
seals have always been regarded as half human.
It is said that the clan MacCodrum had affinity
with the seals, and at the time of the annual seal
battue in autumn an old woman of the clan
was always seized by violent pains out of sympathy with her kinsfolk of the sea that were

then being murdered at their surf-drenched island home. On one island the destruction of the seals continues, and only the year before my first visit to that isle the grey seals had been attacked by a crew of crofter-fishermen who killed many helpless pups and sailed away with their craft deep loaded. There is no doubt that a more strict enforcement of the Grey Seals' Protection Act would save the lives of many seal pups and their mothers. But one must in fairness remember that the destruction of the grey seals is not an act of senseless slaughter. The crofters and fishermen boil down the thick layer of fat which is present on every Atlantic seal. The oil thus obtained is excellent nourishment for cattle and is mixed with their winter feed. The skins of the seals are cured and are made into waistcoats and into the sporrans worn with the kilt.

In the old days portions of the seals were eaten by the islesmen. The meat smelt so strongly that it was conveyed to the mouth on long sticks in order that the hands should not come in contact with it.

Amongst fishermen the seals are, to say the least of it, unpopular, and there is no doubt that they do kill salmon and sea-trout, besides cod and other sea-fish. But the seals prey upon dog-fish also, and every fisherman knows that dog-fish are the riff-raff of the ocean, tearing the herring-nets, eating the hooks baited for cod, ling, and other deep-swimming fish, and making themselves thoroughly objectionable.

Atlantic seals haunt Skerryvore, an isolated rock on which a lighthouse stands west of the Island of Tiree. Sometimes of an evening the lightkeepers fish for big pollack from Skerry-vore, and I heard an amusing story of how a great seal one night seized the fly and threatened, before the line broke, to drag rod and angler into the water.

In the old days there lived in the Isle of Mull a hunter called Donnachda Donn, or Brown Duncan. This hunter owned a famous musket, with which he killed three deer with one shot in Glen Clachaig.

One day shortly before his death Duncan unfortunately shot at a mermaid which he mistook for a seal. The mermaid thereupon laid a spell upon hunter and musket, and when next Duncan fired his gun it burst, and Duncan did not long survive it.

A HEBRIDEAN STORM

In late autumn the Outer Hebrides are often the home of almost continual storms.

Here, one is on the rim of ocean, and from the wild misty spaces of the Atlantic westerly gales hurry over green sullen waters from which the spindrift is caught up in white clouds.

The mornings are long in breaking, these dark November days, and in the darkest hour that precedes the dawn one hears the driving hail upon the window and the rushing of the eager wind. Grey daylight reveals a storm-swept world. Upon North Uist (the island from which I write) no trees grow, but the gale shakes the small bushes that surround the lodge. Tree-sparrows—it is a curious thing that on the treeless Outer Hebrides the tree-sparrow should be more numerous than on the mainland—cower in these storm-swept bushes, seeking what shelter they can from the salt-laden wind.   Across the small lochs white-crested wavelets hurry.

Along the coast a mountainous sea is running.   On the western horizon enormous waves are breaking upon the rocky Isle of Haskeir, and their drifted spray rises to a height of fully a hundred feet.   Around the primitive crofting village of Houghary there is much activity.   During the summer, bad weather has been almost continuous, and now it is November and the oats, rye, and barley are still unsecured.   Never has so late a harvest been known.   Already the crofters have lost a portion of their crop, for a fierce gale lifted the sheaves and blew some of them into the Atlantic.   And so the men and women of the village are now busy carrying large stones into the fields to hold down their sodden harvest.   With great labour the scattered sheaves are collected and are tied together with ropes weighted with stones. But some of the crop has been blown so far that it lies in pools of water, or upon the road, and it is impossible to tell who is the owner of these stray sheaves.

From the spray-drenched shore most of the birds have been driven. A young solan goose lies dead on the shingle. From its nesting-cliff on Saint Kilda, fifty miles to the west, it but recently took its first flight from its nest, and incessant heavy seas dashed its life from it. Its body now lies upon the beach, the wings half spread and the bill open as though in mute protest.

Dimly, through the blinding spray, a flock of long-tailed duck can be seen swimming amongst the breakers. At the oncoming of each wave they dive with a flick of the wings, and seem little inconvenienced by the storm. Ringed plover and turnstones are standing at the margin of a freshwater pool a few hundred yards from the sea. The storm is so fierce that they are unable even to feed, and stand patiently, head to wind, awaiting the abatement of the gale.

Westward a cloud of inky blackness is forming. It increases in size and speeds forward ominously. Flanking it are green skies and white, towering *cumulus* clouds, and beneath it the sea is black as night.

Soon the storm reaches the shore. Hail falls in torrents. The large hailstones are travelling at a speed little short of a mile a minute, and it is impossible for any living thing to face their furious onslaught. Green plover and redshank fly uncertainly this way and that, seeking shelter. The crofters have vanished from their fields, and the squall is so terrific that it is impossible to see their houses less than half a mile away.

Although it is noon twilight covers the isle; sea, hills, and sky are hidden in white driving vapours.

The storm is long in passing, but at last a rift shows in the clouds westward, and the air gradually clears. Ponderously, with vast force, the great Atlantic waves break far out to sea in a cloud of foam on a submerged reef of rocks; the small Island of Causamul is swept constantly by the spray of breaking waves.

Suddenly, from the boiling surf of a rocky cove, the long retriever-like head of a grey seal is thrust into the air. Swimming horizontally in manlike attitude, the seal suspiciously eyes the wayfarer on the shore at a distance of a hundred yards. It is heedless of the lesser seas that strike it, but sinks beneath the water just as some great wave threatens to break upon it. Several times it disappears and emerges, then swims oceanward into a seething waste of waters, and is seen no more.

On a rocky headland purple sandpipers stand, and snipe crouch low in the shelter of small ledges of rock, lying so close that one almost treads upon them.

All bird-life is in the grip of the storm, and is fighting for its very existence.

THE SANDERLING: AN AUTUMN VISITOR TO THE ISLES

Sanderling nest beyond the Arctic circle and visit our shores on migration. From August until November they may be seen in little companies on sandy shores, but almost all of them pass beyond Britain to winter in more southerly lands. In its autumn plumage the sanderling is not unlike the dunlin, but is much lighter in colour, for its under parts, breast, and neck are snowy white.

On the western shores of the Outer Isles long stretches of sandy shores lie, with little bays where the ebbing tide deposits a layer of seaweed. Many birds are on these fair shores. Here are to be found sanderlings, turnstones, ringed plover, redshank, bar-tailed godwits, and curlew, while overhead whimbrel often pass with shrill twittering cry.

It was one Sunday evening in late August that I saw the first sanderling, newly arrived from the Arctic. A strong westerly breeze was bringing in a confused sea, and the tide was very high. The machair was bright with flowers as I crossed to the Atlantic. On the drier levels were blue fields of gentians ; blue fields of scabious grew where the ground was damper. And over the whole machair were spread the sturdy plants and small flowers of the eye-bright. How delightful are these fields of blossom ! In their colouring they match the azure zenith, where snowy *cumulus* clouds idly float, and the immense Atlantic plains that are so near.

Other blooms one finds upon the machair these late August days, but they are more scattered. Above the surrounding grasses the chicory raises its long sturdy stem that bears several large aster-like flowers of a very charming blue. The knapweed is still in bud, and along the sandy beaches, just out of reach of a high tide, the sea-lavender still blooms. Here and there great clusters of ragwort throw a flame of gold across the machair, and a few blossoms of bird's-foot trefoil and wild pansy still show

where a month previously they had covered the
earth with a wealth of bloom.

It is a peculiarity of the sanderling that they
feed chiefly at the height of the tide, and this
August day I saw, unexpectedly, at the edge of
the waves, a company of these delightful birds
feeding actively. In the strong light a telescope
brought them very near, showing the white
breast and under parts, the delicately coloured
back with its greyish-brown feathers, and the
black legs and bill. Individual birds of the
flock retained the dark brown of the breeding
plumage. One of the small visitors was unusually active, and followed up each receding
wave, feverishly picking up the minute animal-
life which the wave had deposited on the sand.
After a time, its appetite satisfied, it ran into
the sea and had a bathe, throwing the water
over its head and back and flapping its
wings vigorously. Its bath over, it rose
lightly from the water with a flutter of wings
and alighted beside a mass of seaweed that
acted as a natural breakwater against the waves.
It dried itself, rubbing its breast and flanks
carefully with the back of its head, and then
made an elaborate toilet, preening each feather

11

carefully. Sheltering behind the seaweed the sanderling now attempted to doze, but the waves of the oncoming tide disturbed it and caused it frequently to change its position. At last it seemed to decide that sleep under the circumstances was impossible, and philosophically commenced to feed once more.

This bird and its fellows waded into the waves thigh-deep, and when a larger wave than usual swept in upon them, they rose on fairylike wings and hovered a foot or two above the water. Only once did I see a sanderling show annoyance with another of the flock, and it drove off angrily a neighbour that approached its beat too closely.

Two days later I again visited the shore as the flood-tide swept in from the west. The wind blew strong from the north-west and a heavy swell broke on the lonely shore. It was not long before I located the sanderling. They were feeding with supreme grace and at incredible speed. Each wave left behind it a line of froth, and along this line the sanderling were feeding, picking up with lightning swiftness objects so tiny as to be invisible to me. Later on in the day I examined one of the frothy lines, and found in it innumerable minute amber-coloured worms or larvæ. These wee creatures were so delicate, that when I placed them on my finger and held them exposed to the air for a few minutes they dried up and lost their form.

That night the Atlantic was of a wonderful tone of spiritual blue. As I lay hidden at the edge of the dunes a tide of varied bird-life flowed unsuspectingly past me. Steering for Saint Kilda, solan geese, sometimes singly, sometimes in pairs, passed a little way offshore. As they flew they constantly scanned the agitated waters beneath them for herring or mackerel. Anon their incredibly keen vision spied a fish far below. Followed a sudden pause in the flight, then a headlong descent and a quick plunge that sent up a fountain of spray. When the solans hunt in pairs both birds sometimes dive simultaneously, often entering the water only a few feet from one another, yet never colliding. Fishing as they go, they fly straight into the setting sun, towards a magic gateway that seems for a few fleeting minutes thrown open to reveal to mortal eyes the glory of Tir nan Og. On the long swell small flocks of scoter ducks rode buoyantly.

In their jet-black plumage with yellow bill the scoter drakes are handsome beside their mates, dressed in sober-coloured brown. They too, like the sanderling, had newly arrived on Hebrid seas from northern haunts.

Often during that autumn I saw the sanderling. One October day, when the sun was warm and a gentle breeze from the west just stirred the grasses of the machair, many of these birds were feeding on the shore, and with them ringed plover, oyster-catchers, and turnstones. Over the sea a skein of geese passed south. As they crossed Causamul they swerved for a moment and hesitated in their flight; but continuing their southward journey, they were soon abreast of the Monach Isles, and then were lost on the horizon as they hurried southward towards Barra, or perhaps grassy Islay and the Irish coast beyond it.

In a sheltered bay a number of long-tailed ducks were swimming. The handsome drakes, conspicuous in their black and white plumage, were holding erect the two long tail-feathers which have given the bird one of its local names, "sea-pheasant," and were swimming excitedly round their sober-coloured ducks as though in courtship. Gradually the ducks drifted inshore and commenced to dive for food only a few feet from the dry sand. After a time the drakes swam in and joined them, but they were uneasy so close to the shore and after a few minutes swam out to deeper water.

Amongst the sanderling was feeding to-day a small bird with red-brown plumage and bill curved curlew-fashion. After a time the curlew-sandpiper—for such it seemed to be—flew gracefully away.

By the shore was a ringed guillemot in sad plight. Its breast-feathers had been matted by crude oil (which nowadays is such a menace to bird-life on the seas), and the bird was so sick that it was unable to fly or even enter the water.

As evening came, and over the Atlantic great *cumulus* clouds gathered, a flock of wild swans flew overhead, moving swiftly down from the north. They passed with loud-toned honking cries, and then there was silence once more along the shore of the sanderling, where the flood-tide made soft music as it crept across the long white sands of Uist an Eorna.

One's thoughts then turned to the "rune" gathered by that scholarly man and lover of the Isles and their people, the late Alexander Carmichael :

> " Mar a bha,
> Mar a tha,
> Mar a bhitheas,
> Gu brath.
> A Thrithinn
> Nan gras,
> Ri traghadh,
> 'S ri lionadh.
> A Thrithinn
> Nan gras,
> Ri traghadh,
> 'S ri lionadh."

> " As it was,
> As it is,
> As it shall be,
> Evermore.
> O Thou Triune
> Of Grace,
> With the ebb,
> With the flow.
> O Thou Triune
> Of Grace,
> With the ebb,
> With the flow."

HARVEST-TIDE

THE south wind blows softly, bringing on the quiet October air the tang of seaweed from the low Atlantic shore a mile away. Around the lodge tree-sparrows cluster upon the stunted bushes, and corn-buntings are perched amongst the sparrows. In a field close by redwings, newly arrived from overseas, are feeding, and twites twitter as they pass overhead in compact flocks.

It is late October, yet the sun is warm, the sea is serene and blue, and many insects dance above the machair that is beside the Atlantic. The tide is low. Upon the wet sands many birds are feeding—dunlin, ringed plover, and turnstones—and from time to time with fast, wheeling flight they change their feeding-grounds. Across the glistening sands an old herdsman, whose only language is the Gaelic, is driving the cattle of the neighbouring crofters to the common grazing; by the shore men are reaping with the scythe the long bent grass used for the thatching of the corn-stacks.

There has been heavy weather of late in the Atlantic, and the sandy shore is uniformly covered with seaweed to a remarkable depth. In places a solid wall of sea-ware about four feet in height is played upon by the waves. Here a great company of sea-gulls and a number of ravens are searching for food, and from a stranded whale near by a small flock of great black-backed gulls rise and flap heavily out to sea.

At the edge of the flowing tide a purple sand-piper is feeding upon invisible life on the surface of some seaweed that is gently swayed with each wave.

Above the machair many larks pour, as at spring-tide, a flood of joyous music from the blue vault of heaven, and many lapwings pass overhead, twinkling like stars as the sun momentarily shines upon their light under-plumage as rhythmically they move their wings. Ravens constantly patrol the shore. They are present in such numbers that one imagines they must be, in part, migrants from northern lands—perhaps from Shetland or the Faroes, or farther afield, from Scandinavia. One of the ravens, finding some delicacy among the heaped-up seaweed, rises into the air with it and, soaring on the breeze, pecks at its prize as it flies.

The seaweed that everywhere lies so thickly is chiefly the common laminarian weed—a long, smooth stem bearing at its apex a broad perforated " leaf." A more uncommon variety which one sees here and there has the stem curiously inrolled and the " holdfast " (which in seaweeds takes the place of a root) wrinkled and bulbous. The scientific name of this laminarian is *Saccorhiza bulbosa*, and sometimes it attains a length of six feet, with the bulb at the base as large as a man's head.

On the calm sea a pair of great northern divers are swimming and diving. After a time one of them emerges with a large flounder grasped in its bill. Long and arduous are the efforts of the bird to swallow its catch. At last, after repeated shakings and bitings, the fish is sufficiently pliable to be swallowed whole, and the diver complacently shakes itself, dips its bill several times in the water, then dives to search for fresh victims.

A scoter drake in glossy black plumage flies

low over the sea, and godwits call musically as
they cross the shore to their feeding-ground.
At the edge of the beach flocks of twites are
feeding upon the seeds of the sea-lavender,
twittering softly to each other as they daintily
extract the seeds from the capsules.

Many shells lie upon the firm, hard shore.
Very beautiful are those of the transparent
limpet (*Helcion pellucidum*). They are small and
fragile, with lines of blue so delicate that they
match the distant waters of the ocean or the
sky at the zenith.   Here and there are stranded
the egg-cases of the dog-fish—capsules of oblong
shape which have been washed by the heavy waves
from the submerged forests of the sea to which
their tendrils were coiled.   These egg-cases
are creamy white, and thus at a glance can be
distinguished from the black egg-cases of the
thorn-back ray, which are also plentiful upon
Hebridean shores.

As the sun sinks westward a wandering solan
momentarily reflects the soft glow as it glides
low above the waves.

Another day of harvest-tide that I recall
followed a night when the west wind rushed
across the Isles from the misty spaces of the

Atlantic. But with the dawn came a calm, and at sunrise each island loch lay with glassy surface in the windless air. Above each lochan a layer of thin grey mist floated, and away to the south the hills of South Uist were wrapped about in soft clouds so that only the summits appeared—seeming like ethereal isles set in a fairy sea.

Almost before the dew had left the grass the crofters commenced to lead in their corn. From the township by the sea at sunrise might have been seen a procession of carts crossing to the machair. Here was land that had been sown for the first time the previous spring; the reaped oats had been built up into small stacks on the fields, there to dry sufficiently to be carted home to the stackyards.

Harvesting is tedious work when crop and stackyard are separated by two miles of rough road, and since in the Isles the carting is done by ponies the carts are small, and less grain can be carried at a load than on the mainland.

At noon the sun shone from a cloudless sky. Ravens with deep croak flew high overhead; through the cobalt fields of the sky a falcon sailed in spirals. From the east came many bird-voices, and high overhead a flight of grey geese passed, steering westward toward the ocean.

Along the low shores the Atlantic swell was breaking. In the sunlight the sands of the Monach Isles shone, and a boat steering from those lonely islands to the Country (as North Uist is locally named) had to depend upon her oars, for in the unwonted calm her sail was useless. North-west rose Haskeir's rocky flanks. Here great fountains of glistening water leaped into the air as the enormous waves threw themselves unwearyingly in endless succession against this lonely outpost of the Isles.

Faintly and mysteriously the isles of Saint Kilda rose from the rim of ocean, a full fifty miles out into the Atlantic. Here are Boreray with great precipices where thousands of solans nest, and Hirta where the little community of less than fourscore persons have their home, cut off from the outside world from September until June—when the first steamer reaches them.

There is an old tradition that in a past age dry land extended west from Uist and Harris as far as Saint Kilda, and that the Princess of Harris with her greyhounds hunted deer over all the wide spaces that are now Atlantic deeps.

It is known that the sea is indeed encroaching on the Isles, for it is on record that moss, trees, and masonry have been brought up by anchors from a full twenty fathoms of water. And at low tide in certain places the stumps of ancient forests may be seen projecting above the sand. Now there are no trees on the Isles. They were burnt, it is said, by a witch sent at the bidding of a Norse princess. This princess had married a prince of the Lewes, but he forsook her and married a maid of the Isles, and it was to avenge herself upon him that the slighted princess caused the woods to be destroyed.

Two hours after midday a breeze drifted in from the ocean. Many larks poured down to earth a murmur of song. Out to sea showers formed, and drifted on the breath of the breeze towards the land. At sunset the clouds were golden, and seaward the colouring was too wonderful to describe. Heskeir nan Ron became a purple isle. Faint blue were the peaks of Saint Kilda. From the wild reef known as Dureberg beyond the Monach Isles a cloud of spray drifted slowly down wind, and in the setting sun the spray seemed like the glowing smoke of some vast fire on Atlantic waters.

SEA-TROUT OF THE ISLES

IT was the 30th of October and the last day but
one of the sea-trout fishing in the Outer Isles.
All through the night heavy rain had fallen
and each burn was in spate.

The morning sun shone warm; in the clear
air the loch mirrored the idly drifting clouds.
Amongst the close-cropped heather the lousewort still showed its red flowers; here and there
were blue scabious blossoms untouched by wind
and rain.

From beside the loch came the thrice-repeated
whistle of a wandering greenshank—a delightful
note that is heard only in wild and wind-swept
acres, and even there but rarely.

The sky was full of colour. Great *cumulus*
clouds of pale grey or snowy white were herded
slowly eastward by the fitful breeze. Here and

there they emptied their showers upon the land or upon the grey plains of the Atlantic. Where the sky was cloudless the heavens, that to-day seemed a greenish blue, showed themselves.

From the mouth of the loch a heavy volume of dark peat-stained water was making its way to the sea less than half a mile distant, and in those dark waters many sea-trout were doubtless forcing their way upstream.

A great reed-bed extends into the loch from its northern shore. Here a flock of redwings were resting. They had, mayhap, newly arrived from the birch forests of Scandinavia, where they nest beyond the Arctic circle. When alarmed they flew restlessly this way and that, disturbing a snipe, which in the old Gaelic tales is one of the *siant* or bespelled birds.

A burn enters the loch at its upper end. Its yeasty waters hurry over rocky ledges and form (in heavy spate) a likely sea-trout pool where they join the loch.

Momentarily the breeze dropped lighter, and fish were not showing. The only chance of success seemed to be to fish the broken water where the stream entered the loch. The first time down I felt several sea-trout " take me "

well below the surface, but they "came short,"
and I was beginning to think of changing my
fishing-ground when I felt a hard pull, low
down, and was into a good fish. Time after
time he leaped with supreme grace far out of
the water, and once or twice swam almost
between my legs, for the water was so deeply
coloured he did not see me. At length I had
him tired out and safely into the landing-net—
a clean-run sea-trout of two and a half pounds.

A second try over the same broken water
yielded a second fish. He, too, fought well,
and when landed glistened like a silver bar in
the October sunlight. This sea-trout had left
the Atlantic not many hours previously, for
several of those marine crustacea, popularly
known as sea-lice, were still biting into his
silvery scales. For his weight—just one and a
half pounds—he was one of the most perfectly
proportioned sea-trout I have seen, thick and firm
with very small head, and that pale greenish tinge
on the back that is seen only on clean-run fish.

Northward dark clouds had spread across
the sky, and as the tail of a passing shower
just touched the loch the breeze momentarily
freshened, then shifted from south to west.

But soon the wind dropped to a light air, and then even the light air was gone, so that the loch lay like a sheet of glass in the sunlight, which seemed a gift of August rather than October.

Above the moor three ravens soared in spirals, scanning the ground beneath them.

From high in the heavens came the clamour of wild geese, and a great company of seventy or eighty of these birds crossed over, their course south-east. With heavy flight a heron passed above the loch; a flock of green plover moved in close attendance upon an immature black-backed gull.

In late October the days are short. Just before five o'clock the sun sank, a ruddy ball, beneath the distant ocean horizon, and for an instant before disappearing shed a rosy glow across all the fair country of this western isle. A billowy cloud to the east was all at once diffused with soft salmon-pink light; in the waters of the loch the pale sky above was coldly reflected. Suddenly a vast flock of starlings, flying in close-packed, well-ordered formation, descended precipitately upon the reed-bed, and a confused murmur, as of a river in spate, was

12

heard as each of those thousands of birds, grasping with its claws the reed stems, held converse before settling down for the night. Did the human onlooker move, the strange volume of sound ceased abruptly as that part of the flock near to him changed its position, but in a few seconds the bird-talk was renewed. Here and there a sea-trout broke the surface of the darkening loch, but the breeze held off, and fishing was useless.

After sunset a chill came to the air. For long, upon the western horizon, the clouds were delicately tinged with pink, and, mingling with the sunset, the periodic flashes of the Monach light lit up the rim of ocean. In the evening air was the smell of peat fires; and when the last of the sunset had faded, a short-eared owl, rising from beside the road, flew with silent, ghostly flight out towards the southern sky where the new moon, sickle-shaped and incredibly slender, shone pale upon a land of wild beauty.

SUMMER SHIELINGS

In bygone days the summer shieling was an integral part of the life of the Highlands and islands of Scotland. But like many others of the old customs it has disappeared—entirely from the mainland and almost entirely from the Isles.

To see summer shielings occupied, and to see shieling life, one must go to Lewis, the most northerly of the Outer Hebrides, for only on this island does the old custom survive.

Here the common grazing in some communities is not sufficiently fertile or extensive to feed the cattle during the whole year. It is arranged, therefore, to close the grazing for a certain period each summer, and during that period the cows are taken to the moorlands to be pastured there, and the people tending their stock live in small primitive dwellings reached by means of a rough moorland track, and often far from the nearest village.

Summer shielings are occupied only so long as the common grazing is closed. Some communities close their grazing for five, some for six, others for eight weeks. By the end of July the shieling season is over and the people return to their homes.

There is romance in shieling life. How delightful must it be to set out for the moorlands on a fine June morning with one's dog and one's cattle, and live the simple life during the two finest months of the year! Long may the old custom continue.

It was late one evening when a friend and I reached the country of the shielings. The air was still, and here and there across the moor the blue peat smoke from the shielings rose into the air. My friend knew the inmates of one of the shielings, and as he conversed with them in Gaelic it was evident that we were expected to pass the night with our hosts, who insisted on giving up their dwelling to us and removing to the shieling of a neighbour.

The sun set, and the cows were herded in and were tethered around the wee house. On the horizon could be seen cattle being driven home to neighbouring shielings : here and there boys and girls were talking together, and perhaps discussing the arrival of the strangers. The peat fire was fanned into flame, and we sat down to a wonderful meal of eggs and bacon, scones, newly churned butter, and sweet cheese of which the Gaelic name is *gruth*. After supper there was much piping and dancing on the rough moorland outside, and as the moon rose golden in the east there was the singing of old Gaelic songs, such as Crodh Chailein and Fhir a' Bhata.

The peat fire flickered brightly, the two stools were as comfortable as many an armchair in more pretentious surroundings. Girlish voices singing the old songs with a lilt in them in the gloaming seemed to carry one back to things of a past age—to the days when Tearlach Og, Prince Charles Edward, sought sanctuary in the Long Island after his defeat. Only that afternoon we had visited a house upon the island of Scalpay on which the following inscription was written above the door :

" Air an laraich so bha an tigh anns do chuir Prionnsa Tearlach seachad gu h-allabanach cuid de laithibh mar fhogarrach 'na rioghachd dhlighich fein."

" On this foundation was the house in which Prince Charles as a wanderer passed some days as a fugitive in his rightful kingdom."

Summer-time finds no favour in the Isles, and it was after midnight when the *ceilidh* came to an end and we were left alone in the shieling.

Through the hole in the roof the blue smoke curled upward ; outside could be seen the dim forms of the cattle as they lay upon the heather. The shieling was larger than most, and, instead of the usual heather couch, possessed an excellent bed. Above the bed was another hole in the roof, which gave ventilation and which could be closed in wet weather. The walls were thick : the roof of turf rested upon a wooden framework. Each year the shielings are roofed anew, for the " thatch " is not built to stand the winter storms.

Every summer shieling has two entrances. They are not doors in the usual sense of the word, but are openings in the walls of the house. Let us imagine the wind is blowing from the

east.   Then the east entrance is closed with turf
and wood and the western "door" is opened ;
if during the day the wind shifts, then the
"doors" are changed.   But at any time of the
day or night one entrance is always open, for
there are no windows to light those small
summer houses.

Early next morning the sun, shining through
the open doorway, flooded the shieling with
golden light.   It was impossible to lie long
abed under such conditions, and for an hour
before breakfast the "songs" (as they say in the
west) of the pipes carried far across the moor.
More peats were carried in, the fire (which is
not allowed to die out during the night) was
soon burning brightly, and we were not long
in sitting down to a breakfast which we shall
always remember.   During the night the wind
had shifted, and so the alternate entrance was
opened before breakfast and had the effect of
changing the whole appearance of the shieling.
The breath of heather entered the room with
the wind ;   the moorland grasses waved and
nodded, and there were wavelets upon the stream
with deep peaty pools that flowed near.   Upon
the hills of Harris southward the clouds rose and

fell, and on the western horizon were the hazy Atlantic plains, where ceaselessly the swell broke upon the outlying isles in a smother of misty spray.

That very evening shieling life would end for the year and the people would return to their homes—glad, perhaps, to see their friends again, but sorry to leave the heather-scented moorland and the lochs on which the moonbeams play during the hours of the short summer night.

THE TRAGEDY OF A GREAT FROST

In the Sound of Harris are many islands. Some of these isles are large, and are inhabited by a population of Gaelic-speaking crofters and fishermen. On others sheep are pastured, and upon one at least the red deer is still to be found. The sentinels of this island group are mere rocks against which the Atlantic surf breaks tirelessly, and upon one of the most outlying of these rocks is the roosting-place of hundreds, perhaps thousands, of shags.

The shag or green cormorant is a voracious feeder. Twice daily he fills himself with fish (chiefly small saithe), and after each meal flies heavily back to his rock, there to rest and dry his wings until the cravings of hunger urge him forth to hunt once more beneath the green waters.

185

One sunny winter day when the air was of that soft clearness so characteristic of the Isles, I sailed across the Sound of Harris and passed close to the resting-place of the green cormorants.   The birds had breakfasted, and crowded together on the flat top of their rock.   So close did they press one upon the other that each inch of the rock was occupied.   With solemn gaze the great black-plumaged company watched the passing of the boat.

It was then that an old fisherman in the boat recalled the tragedy of the rock of the green cormorants.

Many years ago, he said, a great frost gripped the Isles.   In the Outer Hebrides frost is usually a fleeting thing, but that winter the temperature was so low that the wild swans were frozen upon the lochs and even the Atlantic had an icy margin.

Day after day, in the clear sunny weather, the green cormorants could be seen fishing in the Sound, and at dusk winging their way to their lonely rock amid the sleepless seas.

At length came a night when the frost was so numbing that the crofters at their peat fires could find little warmth; when the springs were bound with black ice and above the Atlantic a layer of frozen mist hung.

Next day the fishermen of the Sound of Harris, as they lifted their creels, remarked upon the absence of green cormorants from the sea. The waters were so calm that the birds should certainly have been visible upon them, since the other winter visitors to the Sound were there as usual. Long-tailed drakes, with tail-feathers jauntily curled, were riding buoyantly on the lazy swell, or else were diving with a flick of the wings to their feeding-ground upon the ocean bed, and great northern divers were beside them. But of the *scarbh* or green cormorant there was no sign. Day succeeded day, and always the shags were absent from their accustomed fishing-grounds. Then one morning—since the weather remained calm and settled—a boat sailed out to the remote resting-place of the green cormorants in order to set lobster creels about it.

As they neared the rock the boat's crew began to be aware of the extraordinary tragedy that had befallen the cormorants—a tragedy so weird as to be almost unbelievable. The rock indeed was peopled with its birds as usual, but as the craft sailed close in the bird company remained motionless ; it was as though they were be-spelled.   As they looked more closely the fisher-men began to note something unusual in the attitude of many of the birds, and to wonder what had befallen the dark-plumaged clan. It was only on landing upon the rock itself that the full extent of the tragedy was realised. Over all the small rocky isle lay, in grotesque attitudes, hundreds of dead cormorants.   Their feet were chained to the rock, and their most desperate efforts had failed to liberate them.

Straight from their last fishing they must have flown to the rock one evening of intense frost. Their feet when they arrived had been damp from the sea, and as they slept the frost bound them with iron clasp.   One can picture the scene next morning.   The cormorants on awakening discovered to their dismay that they were unable to fly to their fishing-grounds, and from the rock must have come a wild chorus of harsh, terrified cries that drifted unheeded across the lonely sea.   Day after day the frost continued, and the green cormorants became grad-ually weaker.   One by one they sank exhausted, and the sleep of death overtook them until the very last of that great assembly left its imprisoned body and flew swiftly in the spirit to the unseen isles beyond the ocean horizon where is, one likes to imagine, the spiritual world of the sea-birds.

Soon the grey crows, the ravens, and the great black-backed gulls gathered about this rock of the dead. Followed days of feasting, so that when spring at length was come all that remained upon the isle were many bleached bones, many bedraggled feathers, and mummified feet long since liberated from their imprisonment.

This is the story of the tragedy of the green cormorants as I heard it when sailing across a sunlit sea. For years after the event the shag population on these seas was small, but now the feathered fishermen are as plentiful as ever upon their smooth wave-worn rock.

THE ISLES OF THE MONKS

FROM the Atlantic six miles south-west of the
most westerly point of Uist rise Eilean nam
Manach, or the Isles of the Monks, deriving
their name because in the dim past a monastery
stood here.[1]

To Saint Kilda itself a steamer with mails
and passengers makes several calls during the
summer months, but to the Monach Isles
(as the Isles of the Monks are usually named
nowadays) no steamship ever comes, and so the
arrival of strangers is a great event in the lives
of the people.

The Monach Isles consist of two low-lying

[1] In Blaeu's Atlas of 1662 the island group is named
Helskyr na Monich, and a beacon is marked upon it.

grassy islands—Ceann Iar to the west and Ceann n' Ear to the east.   Besides these islands there are two lesser isles.   Of these, Stockay is uninhabited, but on Shillay a lighthouse stands, and each night sends forth white rays that can be seen from the whole chain of the Outer Hebrides.

It is fitting that Shillay (or Seiley) should have been chosen as the site for a lighthouse, for it was on this isle that the kindly monks showed ruddy beacons in the days of long ago to warn passing vessels, or perhaps the " birlinn " of some Highland chief, of their peril.

After the monks had left the isles, but before the time of the lighthouse, the Monach islanders were accustomed to pasture their sheep upon Shillay.   One fine day all the men and women sailed across to shear sheep.   After a time the men left their women-folk on the isle and sailed out to a tidal rock some little distance away to kill grey seals.   But in the excitement of the chase they did not secure their boat properly and it drifted away.   Soon the women realised the peril of their men.   Their cries for help were heard by a woman on the opposite shore.   Single-handed she launched a large boat, but before help could arrive the watching women saw their husbands one by one swept into eternity by the heavy seas that engulfed the rock with the rising tide.

Ceann n' Ear is the only one of the Monach Isles that is inhabited now—if the lighthouse-keepers on Shillay be excepted. On Ceann n' Ear eight families live. The fishermen among them reap a rich harvest from the sea, which yields lobsters, pollack,[1] mackerel, flounders, and saithe.

Twice a week in summer when the weather is kind one of the fishermen sails across to the "mainland" (as the Monach islanders name North Uist) with mails. But in winter there are often continuous gales and strong winds which cut off the island group from the outside world for a month or six weeks at a stretch. How anxiously at such times must the islesmen scan the horizon for a change in the weather, for there is no telegraph on the island group, and they are entirely dependent on the small fishing craft that sails to Uist, dim across the stormy sea on the eastern horizon!

Some years ago came a winter day when

[1] Called *lythe* by the people in the Isles.

the west wind blew with extreme violence. Ceann n' Ear is low, and the tide commenced to rise alarmingly. Great waves, ever increasing, thundered in across the low sandy shore until they swept over the grass of the machair. At length some of the houses themselves were in danger, and in alarm the inhabitants collected on the higher parts of the isle. That day will long be remembered on the Monach Isles, and for some time afterwards the people wished to emigrate to Uist, and at least one family has done so.

One summer morning, when the lightest of southerly airs stirred the grasses of the machair, I crossed from North Uist to the Monach Islands. Slowly the flood-tide crept up the mud-flats of Loch Paible, where was moored the one boat on all the west coast of Uist fit to make the long passage to the Isles of the Monks. The boat's crew consisted of a venerable islesman of distinguished appearance and his son. The old man had no English, and his son was shy of talking in a strange tongue. The family had recently left the Monach Islands to live on North Uist, and their boat, belonging to Ceann n' Ear, was unlike the craft one finds elsewhere in the Hebrides. The boats of the

13

Monach Isles carry two masts and two rather small sails ; the craft of the Hebrides generally have but one mast and one large mainsail.   But it is considered by the men of the Monach Isles that with two comparatively small sails they are able more easily to handle their boat should a squall suddenly arise.

Against the flood-tide we pulled slowly out of Loch Paible, passing the sea-pool with its rocks covered with fucus seaweed.   Off the sandy shore of the ocean terns fished daintily.   There was scarce sufficient wind to fill our sails ; upon the long westerly swell we rocked gently.   Westward the low sands of Monach glistened ; the high tops of South Uist were of that very deep and wonderful blue that portends rain.

The islesmen of Monach say that their home is the nearest inhabited land to Saint Kilda, which shows in clear weather on the far horizon. One summer day some adventurous spirits set sail westward to cross to that distant western land.   For the first twenty miles or so of the voyage all went well, but then bad weather set in swiftly and they were compelled to put about and steer for home.   And so Saint Kilda remains an unknown country to them.

Gradually the coast of North Uist receded. From the machair whence we had come rose the smoke of a kelp fire, mounting slowly in pale spirals into the still air.   Around the boat solans fished and terns flew gracefully.   Despite our two sails, the oars had to be kept going to help us on our way, and ever the elusive isles ahead of us seemed to recede rather than to approach.

Around the sun now appeared a wide luminous ring that showed in it all the colours of a rainbow.   A ring round the sun is one of the surest prophets of bad weather that I know, and noting it, our veteran boatman prophesied, " Uisge mor," which means " Much rain." (Sure enough, at daybreak next morning half a gale of wind with lashing rain swept the seas.)

Above the sea a stormy petrel fluttered.   It was no larger than a swallow, and its flight had the same buoyant grace.   It is believed by those learned in the lore of the sea that to see a stormy petrel in full daylight is a sign of the approach of bad weather, for " Mother Carey's Chicken " is a nocturnal bird, and sleeps upon the green waters during sunny hours.

Now that we were out at sea, North Uist was spoken of amongst the crew as " the country."

Could this have been the survival of the old custom never, when at sea, to mention one's destination by name, lest the unfriendly spirits that often hover about a boat should overhear, and by summoning a contrary wind should prevent the sailors from reaching their destination?

At last, after a five hours' passage, the ocean swell lessened and we sailed into a sheltered bay, where a number of boats, each with its two distinctive masts, were at anchor.

A small crowd of persons had assembled on the sandy shore to witness the arrival of the strangers. The people seemed strong and healthy, and one was impressed by their prosperous appearance. They were well dressed, and most of them had an excellent knowledge of English. The children as they played on the beach were unusually attractive and handsome.

The houses on Monach are superior to many on North Uist. This is a tribute to the energy of the islesmen, for all the building material must be brought in boats from North Uist across stormy miles of ocean. On the island is a school, and at the time of our visit twelve children were attending it. A stranger

could hardly be persuaded to live here, and so
the education authorities are wise in appointing
a woman of the island as the teacher. At the
time of our visit the summer holidays were
just about to end, for the summer vacation that
year was shortened by a week in order that the
children might have an extra week's holiday
later on to assist at the ingathering of the
harvest.

Shortly after our arrival two islesmen landed
with a "bag" of cormorants, which the people
assured us made excellent eating when skinned.
Other boats were busy at the lobster-fishing,
which is carried on around the island group
whenever the weather is favourable. The
lobsters, which are of large size and excellent
quality, are kept alive in floating-boxes in the
sea until it is possible to send them over to
Lochmaddy in North Uist. Thence they are
sent by steamer and train to market in distant
London.

The Monach Isles are small but fertile.
There is excellent grazing for cattle and horses
on Ceann n' Ear—the inhabited island—and also
on the adjoining isle of Ceann Iar.

The sea between these islands is shallow, and

at low tide it is possible to ride from one to the other.

The boat on which the animals are taken over to North Uist to the sales is a special one. It is not used for fishing and has a single mast.

It was late afternoon as we stood on the machair beside the little loch on which many ducks swam and where women were busy at their washing. Looking to the north, east, and south, one saw rising above the sea a magnificent amphitheatre of hills that seemed to guard this lonely island group. So clear was the air that it was difficult to realise the leagues of ocean that lay between the islands and the sentinel peaks. Upon Eaval heavy rain was falling, but behind it the hills of Skye were clear, and even the distant peaks of Rhum showed themselves. Far to the south were the heights of Barra and Mingulay.

Across the machair bees darted or sucked the honey from the clover. By the tide turnstones twittered and redshanks fluted, and overhead a raven passed.

One looked across to the lighthouse upon Shillay. There can be few island lighthouse

stations so lonely as this one. On a station
officially designated an "island" station, the
lightkeepers and their families must remain
without relief summer and winter. Were
Shillay converted into a "rock" station (as
seems possible as I write), the lightkeepers,
as at the Bass Rock, Skerryvore, and other
"rock" stations, would have a fortnight ashore
for every month spent upon their island home.
The watching on Shillay must be rendered
still more lonely because of the scarcity of
passing vessels, since the isles are out of the
main track of shipping.

Before we set sail on the return journey to
Uist we sat down to a wonderful tea: drop
scones, newly made and light as a feather,
freshly churned butter with the scent of the
flowers of the machair in it, and the richest
of sweet cream.

The islesfolk vied with each other in offer-
ing us hospitality, and it was apparent how
proud they were of their island home. The
question first put was almost invariably, "How
do you like this island?" But even in August
their thoughts were of the winter storms, for
their second remark was usually, "A nice place

—in summer." At length we set sail, and the old music of the Highland pipe accompanied us on our way to Uist. The sea seemed to await in suspense the coming storm. The air was dark and very clear, and away beyond Benbecula the heights of the distant Black Cuillin of Skye rose on the horizon, soft mists clinging to their lower slopes. Beyond Saint Kilda the far western horizon burned with a glorious salmon-pink, and in that transient glow the vast *nimbus* clouds that hung there were transformed to mists of fire.

And as the last of the sunset faded the ponderous Atlantic swell could be seen to crash with stately rhythm upon the great reefs that encircle the lonely Isles of the Monks.

GRIMSAY

NORTHWARD of Iceland, and within the Arctic circle, lies the bleak isle of Grimsey. A frigid ocean upon which icebergs float washes its cliffs, on which many little auks nest.

But far different are the surroundings of Grimsay of the Outer Hebrides, where frost and snow come rarely, and where the air is moist with the spray of the humid Atlantic.

Yet Grimsey of Iceland and Grimsay of the Isles both are Norse for Grim's Island, and, lying so many leagues apart, testify to the restless energy of the conquering race of Vikings of long ago.

The Hebridean Grimsay lies between North Uist and Benbecula. It is a lonely isle, out of the track of the mail steamer. A stranger is rarely seen here, and spinning and weaving occupy the days of the older people. From Carinish in North Uist to Grimsay is a distance of some three miles. The sea between the isles is shallow, and at low tide a great expanse of wet sands with channels of water intersecting them separates Grimsay from Uist, so that a trap can usually drive at the ebb from one island to the other.

A delightful or very stormy drive it can be, according to the mood of the weather. Often screaming redshanks fly above the pony's head, and flights of dunlin and ringed plover wheel and swerve on glistening wings above the sands.

One autumn morning, at the "first of the ford" as they say locally (meaning that the crossing was done at the earliest moment the sea permitted), when the sea in places reached almost to the floor of the trap, I crossed from Uist to Grimsay. The harvest of oats had been gathered in, but in the fields of Uist old women were busy lifting the potatoes. With a sickle-shaped implement known as a *cnocan* the tubers are uprooted in the sandy soil and are collected in pails. The handle of the *cnocan* is only a few inches long, and when using it the people generally kneel on the ground.

Somewhere amongst the pools of brackish

water fringed with sea-thrift a greenshank
made wild continuous music at the edge of
the ford.   Southward, seen dimly through the
haze of fine weather, rose Beinn Mhor and
Hecla of South Uist ;   east towered the shapely
cone of Eaval, most graceful of hills.

So swiftly does the flood sweep in from the
Atlantic at spring-tides that the crossing of
the fords has always in it an element of risk.
Two of the most dangerous fords between the
isles are the North Ford between North Uist
and Benbecula, and the South Ford between
Benbecula and South Uist.

The tragedy of the South Ford, for which
the old Gaelic name is the Ford of the Coming
Storm, is comparatively recent.   After a long
drive across the isles from Lochmaddy in North
Uist, four young men were making their way
over the last ford that lay between them and
their destination, South Uist.   Swiftly streamed
the flood-tide eastward.   Deeper and deeper
around the trap became the water, until at length
the pony, wearied after its long journey, was
unable to go farther.   Three of the men
succeeded in reaching the shore ;   the fourth
was taken by the sea.   The horse, just as its

head disappeared beneath the water, was rescued by a boat.

Then there was the disaster of the North Ford, when, on a dark and foggy night, an exciseman mysteriously disappeared from his trap during the crossing. After this a line of stones was set in the ford to keep the traveller to the track, and although some of these stones have now sunk deep in the sand, others can be seen distinctly.

Grimsay is a primitive island. There is but one road on it, and that leads across to Kallin, a clachan on the south-east side of the isle, overlooking the Minch. At one point the road passes close beside a land-locked bay, beside which stands a lobster-fisher's house. Here a boat can lie safely at her sheltered moorings during the fiercest winter gale, for the entrance to the bay is so narrow that there is scarce room for a boat to steer through it to the open sea beyond.

As one passes the small houses beside the road one sees the women busy at the spinning, but tweed-making is not so thriving an industry as formerly.

When crossing Grimsay toward Kallin, Eaval

of North Uist (1138 feet) rises splendidly to
the east. The name of the hill is Norse,
and its meaning is Island Hill. It doubtless
obtained its name of old because from the sea
it was prominent at a great distance. Eaval
rises abruptly from comparatively level land.
It gives the illusion of some giant wave
that rears itself suddenly from apparently
tranquil deeps on the flanks of some wild
sunken rock.

Rather to the east of Grimsay is a bleak and
rocky island some two miles in length into
which the ocean bites deep. Its name is Ronay,
and formerly a number of crofters dwelt upon
it ; now a shepherd lives alone here.

Martin, writing of this isle in 1700, says
that there is a small chapel upon it named the
Lowlanders' Chapel, " because seamen are buried
here."

Grimsay in autumn gives an impression of
dreariness ; it appears largely a land of bog
and loch, and lacks the fertility and cheerful
atmosphere of the western borders of Uist.
Even the weather that late autumn day
seemed sad upon Grimsay, for it was dark and
misty at noontide, while upon Uist, a few

miles to the north, the sun shone with soft golden light.

The flood-tide was flowing swiftly in from the Atlantic as I crossed again to North Uist that afternoon. In places the water reached to within a couple of inches of the floor of the trap, but the pony, with much experience in the crossing of the fords, was in no way perturbed.

Westward, over Atlantic plains, mist and shade alternated. Faintly to the south Hecla and Beinn Mhor showed, but northward the sky had cleared and the Harris hills, blue and distinct, lay on the northern horizon. The air was warm and still as on a midsummer night, and even after the last of the crimson sunset had faded, many shore birds called as they sped phantom-like overhead to where grey seas broke upon the brink of evening.

THE SEVEN HUNTERS

SOME twenty miles into the Atlantic west of
Gallan Head in the Lewes a group of spray-
swept islands stand. Their name is the Seven
Hunters, or the Flannan Isles, and it is generally believed that they received their name
from Saint Flannan of Cell da-Lua, whose
time was in the seventh century. Saint Flannan
was of a Royal Irish race, the son of Tairdel-
bach, son of Atren, son of Aed, son of
Conall, son of Eochaidh, son of Cairthend,
son of Cass, son of Cormac, son of Conall,
son of Lughaidh, son of Oengus Tirech, son
of Fer Corbb, son of Mogh Corbb, son of
Cormac Cass.

Upon the largest of the Seven Hunters are
still visible the ruins of a chapel, said to have
been dedicated to Saint Flannan, and to the
people of the Lewes this island group has from
earliest times been counted sacred soil, so that

Dean Monro in the sixteenth century speaks
of them as the "haly isles."

At the beginning of the eighteenth century
Martin writes thus of them : "To the north
west of Gallan-head, and within 6 Leagues of it,
lyes the Flannan-Islands, which the Sea-men call
North-hunters ; they are but small Islands, and
six in number, and maintain about 70 Sheep
yearly ; The Inhabitants of the adjacent Lands
of the Lewis, having a right to these Islands,
and visit them once every Summer, and there
make a great purchase of Fowls, Eggs, Down,
Feathers, and Quills : when they go to Sea,
they have their Boat well mann'd, and make
towards those Islands with an East Wind : but
if before, or at the Landing, the Wind turn
Westerly they hoist up Sail, and steer directly
home again.   If any of their Crew is a Novice,
and not vers'd in the Customs of the place, he
must be instructed perfectly in all the Punctilio's
observ'd here, before Landing ; and to prevent
Inconveniences that they think may ensue upon
the transgression of the least Nicety observ'd
here, every Novice is always join'd with another
that can instruct him all the time, of their Fowling ; so all the Boat's Crew are match'd in this

manner : after their Landing they fasten the
Boat to the sides of a Rock, and then fix a
wooden Ladder, by laying a Stone at the foot
of it, to prevent its falling into the Sea ; and
when they are got up into the Island, all of
them uncover their Heads, and make a turn
Sun-ways round, thanking God for their Safety.
The first Injunction giv'n after Landing is, not
to ease Nature in that place where the Boat
lyes, for that they reckon a Crime of the highest
nature, and of dangerous Consequence to all their
Crew ; for they have a great regard to that very
piece of the Rock upon which they first set
their Feet, after escaping the danger of the
Ocean.

" The biggest of these Islands is call'd Island
More, it has the ruins of a Chappel dedicated
to St. Flannan, from whom the Island derives
its Name ; when they are come within about
20 paces of the Alter, they all strip themselves
of their upper Garments at once, and their
upper Clothes being laid upon a Stone, which
stands there on purpose for that use, all the
Crew pray three times before they begin Fowling : the first day they say the first Prayer,
advancing towards the Chappel upon their

14

Knees ; the Second Prayer is said as they go
round the Chappel ; the Third is said hard-by
or at the Chappel, and this is their Morning
Service.   Their Vespers are perform'd with the
like number of Prayers.   Another Rule is, That
it is absolutely unlawful to kill a Fowl with a
Stone, for that they reckon a great Barbarity,
and directly contrary to ancient Custom.

" It is also unlawful to kill a Fowl before they
ascend by the Ladder.   It is absolutely unlawful
to call the Island of St. Kilda (which lyes thirty
Leagues Southward) by its proper Irish Name
Hirt, but only the High Country.   They must
not so much as once name the Islands in which
they are Fowling by the ordinary Name Flannan, but only the Country.   There are several
other things that must not be call'd by their
common Names : E.g. Wisk, which in the
Language of the Natives signifies Water, they
call Burn : a Rock which in their Language
is Creg, must here be call'd Cruey, i.e. Hard :
Shore in their Language exprest by Claddach,
must here be call'd Uah, i.e. a Cave.   They
account it also unlawful to kill a Fowl after
Evening Prayers.   There is an ancient Custom,
by which the Crew is oblig'd not to carry home

any Sheep-suet, let them kill never so many Sheep in these Islands. One of their principal Customs is not to steal or eat anything unknown to their Partner, else the Transgressor (they say) will certainly vomit it up, which they reckon as a just Judgment. When they have loaded their Boat sufficiently with Sheep, Fowls, Eggs, Down, Fish, &c. they make the best of their way homeward. It's observed of the Sheep of these Islands that they are exceeding fat, and have long Horns.

"I heard this superstitious Account not only from several of the Natives of the Lewis, but likewise from two who had been in the Flannan Islands the preceding Year. I asked one of them if he pray'd at home as often, and as fervently, as he did when in the Flannan Islands; and he plainly confess'd to me that he did not: adding further, that these remote Islands were places of inherent Sanctity; and that there was none ever yet landed in them but found himself more dispos'd to Devotion there, than any where else."

This description which Martin wrote over two hundred years ago brings vividly before the imagination the sacred character of these far-flung isles to which the crossing was always a hazardous one, for even if the outward passage were made safely, the landing upon the almost sheer cliff in the heavy Atlantic swell that prevails always here was calculated to test the nerve of the most active and sure-footed men.

The Seven Hunters are still visited by boats from Lewis, but the old observances are fast dying out. Sheep are still pastured here as they were in Martin's day, and there is excellent lobster-fishing for those who are daring enough to risk the long sea passage in their small craft.

At four o'clock of a clear July morning we sailed from Loch Roag in the west of Lewis, and with a following breeze from the south steered for the mouth of the loch. Here we met the heavy Atlantic swell that rolled in with irresistible power from the western ocean, and from now onward we rocked and swayed giddily towards our distant goal. Just off the coast a great assembly of solans were plunging for fish, so that the spray of their diving mingled with the surf that leaped eagerly up the dark rocks. Farther out to sea many small flocks of these birds passed us. With graceful gliding flight they sped low just above the waves, steering for the "High Country,"[1] their nearest nesting-ground.   One flock was led by a youngster—less than a year old and plumaged in dark brown.

At first the Flannan Islands had been invisible in the salt haze.   Gradually they loomed mistily ahead, and as we approached them we could see the two largest isles lying close together with a narrow channel of deep water separating them. The names of these two islands are Eilean Mor or the Big Island, and Eilean Tighe or House Island.   Besides these two there rise from the neighbouring seas smaller rocky isles.   They lift themselves from the foaming waters of the Atlantic, and, although they are small, give nesting sanctuary to myriads of sea-fowl.

The sun was high when at length we sailed into smooth water in the shelter of the great cliffs of Eilean Mor.   To-day the west landing was impossible because of the surf.   At the east landing the sea was smooth, but it was not easy to climb the rock here, even with the help of steps that have been driven into the cliff since the building of the lighthouse.

[1] An old name for Saint Kilda, which was also called Irt nan Caorach Gorma (Saint Kilda of the blue sheep.)

As we emerged on to the sloping crown of the isle we seemed to reach a fairy garden. Here, in all the glory of their bloom, were acres of sea-thrift. The isle was coloured a delicate pink by these countless flowers, and their delightful scent permeated the sea-breeze. Upon the grassy slopes puffins stood in quaint attitudes, or fluttered overhead with bills crammed full of glistening sand-eels for their young. Above us a few great black-backed gulls soared. Well they knew that the young puffins were just hatching, and that the parents were busy carrying food to their families. The lighthouse-keepers told us that when all is quiet a number of these gulls alight near the puffins' burrows. Each great black-back stands patiently outside a burrow. Sooner or later the puffin emerges. The gull swiftly strikes the unsuspecting victim on the back of the head with its powerful bill. Should the first blow miscarry, the puffin has time to face round upon its enemy, and then is usually able to hold its own.

The puffin is not the only bird to suffer from the attacks of this bird criminal, for the great black-backed gull sometimes sweeps down upon the guillemots' ledges, picks up some young

guillemot and swallows it whole.   Such a feat
is not difficult for a bird which was seen on
Eilean Mor to swallow, after a struggle, a half-
grown rabbit.

Here and there in the peaty soil amongst the
puffin burrows one saw the smaller burrows of
the ocean petrels that skim and dart across
the isle in the dusk of a summer night.   These
small petrels are nocturnal in habit, and the
lightkeepers told us that they had never once
seen a single one of these birds in flight in daylight.   At night, during haze or fog (they said),
the petrels often struck the glass of the lantern,
and on one or two occasions disgorged the
contents of the stomach—larvæ about three-
quarters of an inch in length.

From the ruins of Saint Flannan's chapel one
looks west on to a great " stack," upon which
thousands of kittiwakes and guillemots were
clustering this July day.   Over the water graceful fulmar petrels sailed, showing the poetry of
their delightful effortless flight.   Far beneath us
guillemots grunted and groaned as they quarrelled
for space on the whitened ledges where they
clustered like ants.   In rocky crannies rock
pipits tended their young, and half-way down

an almost sheer cliff a dark brown rabbit was feeding amongst a colony of kittiwakes.

So hazardous is the voyage from the Lewes to the Flannans, that there is but one boat that crosses nowadays to fish lobsters. The skipper of this boat is well up in years (as they say in the west). He is a MacDonald, and although a boat of his was once wrecked on the Flannan Isles, he regularly sails the twenty miles of stormy seas in his small craft. That morning we had noticed his boat, anchored securely fore and aft in a sheltered haven, and now we saw him leave his anchorage and hoist sail for the outlying isles. In the vast Atlantic seas the boat staggered and swayed like a drunken thing. And yet the swell—for these wild isles—was by no means heavy, and there must be many days even at midsummer when the little craft is tossed like a cork amid white foaming seas.

In a bay in one of the lesser isles is Poll nan Ron, the Pool of the Seals. Here live bull grey seals of immense size and great age, rivalling in years even the enchanted seal of the Bespelled Isles in the Minch. At the mating season these great bulls fight fiercely, so that the waters of the surrounding sea are dyed crimson.

The breeze freshened. At the edge of the cliffs throngs of puffins crouched in long rows, facing the wind. On the eastern horizon the rugged peaks of Harris rose. Farther south the hills of Uist were faint and of a delicate blue, with clouds resting lightly upon them. But even on this sunny day of summer the Flannan Islands seemed a lonely group. How wild must be the scene and how great the force of the wind at the height of a winter gale!

One winter night a passing vessel saw that the light on Eilean Mor was not lit. On reaching her port she at once reported this, and the relief steamer sailed to the Seven Hunters to investigate. She neared the rock and blew her siren. All was deserted, and so a boat was launched and a landing made.

In the living-room of the tower the tea was set ; the log was written up to a date a few days before, but the light-keepers had mysteriously vanished. Their fate can only be conjectured, but it is believed that they were swept together into the Atlantic by a giant wave, and in the dark seas met a swift and merciful fate.

AN OUTER HEBRIDEAN SHOOT

Nowhere in the British Isles, except perhaps in the west of Ireland, is the shooting so varied and interesting as in the Outer Hebrides. It is certainly true that no record "bags" are to be expected here, and there is endless walking to be done, but the chief delight is that the shooting is full of variety. It is primitive and natural sport, and thus must appeal to all true sportsmen. Sometimes one is up against the weather, and has to face heavy gales that bring in sheets of rain from the Atlantic. At other times the north wind rushes furiously across the Isles, finding its way through many woolly waistcoats, and numbing the hands so that they can with difficulty release the trigger. On these sea-drowned shores the wind is rarely still, but when at last comes a day of serene calm and of blue skies, how delightful a country do the Isles seem—a land of blue skies, blue seas, immense horizons, and keen invigorating air!

The shoot which four of us shared one October was on the fringe of the Atlantic, and from the lodge in clear weather Saint Kilda could be seen standing serenely above the plains of ocean.

Before the war the Outer Isles were fortunate, for at each port a mail-steamer called daily. But the service has now been reduced to three boats a week—the mail-boat sailing from Kyle of Loch Alsh each Monday, Wednesday, and Friday. Besides the mail-boat, the Glasgow steamers *Dunara Castle* and *Hebrides* visit the Isles every ten or eleven days. By leaving Euston or King's Cross on a Sunday evening for Mallaig, and there joining the Outer Isles mail-steamer at noon the following day, it is possible to reach one's destination in the Hebrides the night following one's departure from London. But it is only on a Sunday night that the journey is so short a one, for on her two other trips of the week the mail-boat does not call at Mallaig, but sails from Kyle northward to Harris as her first port of call. And so on these two days the traveller must travel by train from London to Kyle *via* Inverness—a journey of just over eighteen hours.

The sea passage from Kyle or Mallaig to
the Outer Isles is too long to be pleasant in
stormy weather, and it is possible greatly to
shorten the sea voyage by crossing Skye by
road from Kyleakin, opposite Kyle, to Dunvegan on the west of Skye. Here one is in
sight of, and comparatively near to, the Outer
Isles, and from Dunvegan every ten days
the steamer *Hebrides* crosses the Little Minch
to Lochmaddy, no more than thirty miles
distant.

The morning on which we crossed the ferry
from Kyle of Loch Alsh to Skye a fierce gale
was lifting in spindrift the waters of the
sea. During the long drive across to Dunvegan
the gale continued, and there was driving rain all
through the night. Just before daybreak the
wind suddenly dropped to a dead calm, and
when at midday we sailed in the *Hebrides* the
rain had ceased and the sky was clearing. As
we steamed past Dunvegan Head into the Minch
we could see yeasty waterfalls plunging from
the heights over the great cliffs and reaching
the sea in a smother of foam. The sun shone,
and the Minch was calm as a loch. During
our crossing gulls followed us, and one or two

sea-swallows passed the ship, flying south.   On Uist we landed at sunset, after a long row of several miles from the anchorage of the steamer to the landing-place.   It was fortunate for those at the oars that the tide was with us and that there was not a breath of wind.   About us small saithe played, and fishing-boats passed out to the mouth of the loch for the evening fishing.

We found the island sodden with the rain of the previous weeks and the harvest still in the fields.   On the silent air of evening came the deep boom of the Atlantic surf on the western shore of the isle (three miles distant), and far out to sea showed the white rays from the lighthouse upon the Isles of the Monks.

When we awoke next morning we seemed to have miraculously recaptured spring, for larks were mounting high into the serene sky and pouring earthward a flood of song.   Twites, too, made soft twittering music, and tree-sparrows chirruped cheerfully around the lodge.

Our shoot consisted chiefly of snipe ground, on which were also golden and green plover, some duck, and a few grey lag-geese, the last-named birds very wary and cunning indeed.   In

November barnacle geese come in, and sometimes a few white-fronts and brent, but in October they are still in the Arctic.

The fishing for brown trout on the Isles is good. There were several lochs on our shoot where earlier in the season good baskets are made, but the brown-trout season was almost over when we arrived on the island. One of the larger lochs held sea-trout, which ran up from the sea by way of a small peaty burn through the moor. Near our " march " was an excellent sea-trout loch, and a friend was kind enough to give us permission to fish it during the last fortnight of October.

During our stay on the island the weather was never really favourable for the migration of snipe. The home-bred birds usually leave the Outer Hebrides for Ireland in September, and thus from that month onwards one is dependent upon migrants from the north. The best flighting wind in the Isles is a strong breeze from the east, with frost on the mainland, and during our stay the wind blew persistently from west or south-west.

The area of snipe ground was not large, and most of the first " flight " of snipe seemed

lived on it and made frequent raids upon the sea-trout of the loch.

The 20th October was an excellent day among the sea-trout. Although the wind was east and the sky rather hard and clear, the fish for a short time in the morning were really on the take, and for an hour we had splendid sport. One of the party, fishing from the shore with a ten-foot rod, had an exciting twenty minutes with a big fish which took out all his line and most of the " backing." The sea-trout was a beautiful clean-run fish of 4 lb. 2 oz., as silvery as a February salmon. Our total catch that day was twelve sea-trout weighing twenty-two pounds.

It is rare that the weather is too dry for fishing in the Outer Isles in October, but after the 20th of the month scarcely any rain fell, and the lochs soon shrank to summer level. The 29th of the month was wet and stormy and many fish ran up, but the water had not settled before the close of the season on the 31st.

For the bird-lover the Isles are a most attractive country. At the beginning of October neither the great northern diver nor the long-

15

tailed duck had arrived in Hebridean waters,
but during the last week of the month the
duck were feeding in the sandy bays in large
numbers, and the great northern divers were
fishing in deeper waters or were speeding
with powerful flight to distant fishing-grounds.
Even by the beginning of October the solans
were flying well offshore, for the waters of
the Atlantic were fast cooling and the fish
were moving into the depths.

Five whooper swans paid us a visit at the
end of the month. On a day of rain and
strong southerly wind they alighted at flood-
tide on the sea-loch beside the lodge, but
were very suspicious and did not stay long.
They seemed to be a family party consisting
of the parents and three youngsters. Perhaps
they had newly arrived from their nesting-
grounds in Iceland.

During the month one heard often the
wild elusive call of a wandering greenshank.
Sometimes he fluted beside some hill tarn ;
sometimes one disturbed him at his feeding
on the ooze beside a sea-pool at low tide.
There are few bird-calls more wonderful than
the cry of the greenshank. In his voice the

spirit of the wild places lives : his love-song, heard at an immense height above some lonely Highland pine forest in spring, is deathless music that remains in the mind of him who hears it so long as memory lasts.